Veio Pou teaches in the Department of English, Shaheed Bhagat Singh College, University of Delhi. He reads moderately, writes occasionally, and lives in New Delhi with his wife and two daughters. *Waiting for the Dust to Settle* is his first novel.

WAITING FOR THE DUST TO SETTLE

a novel

Veio Pou

SPEAKING
TIGER

SPEAKING TIGER BOOKS LLP
125A, Ground Floor, Shahpur Jat,
New Delhi 110049

First published by Speaking Tiger Books 2020

ISBN: 978-93-89958-52-2
eiSBN: 978-93-89958-53-9

10 9 8 7 6 5 4 3

Typeset in Garamond Premier Pro by SÜRYA, New Delhi
Printed at Chaman Enterprises, New Delhi

I believe that stories are powerful
they have the power to transform lives
the magic to work peace
and then, it is so important that they be told
in any way, even in ways that we have not thought of before
as pictures, as gestures, as dance, as song
in any way they can be told
reinvented, breathing life in new forms
so that they can touch lives and
work their transforming magic.

—Easterine Kire,
'Barcelona Dreamtime'

To all those who have silently endured the pain 'waiting' for the unborn nation, and to those who look to the Lord for justice.

Author's Note

There are situations in life that define the larger society, and there are moments in life that will always be remembered, however unforgiving they may be.

The eighties and the nineties of the last century saw many changes in the socio-political life of the Nagas in particular, and the Northeast of India in general. It was a difficult period of transition. It seemed like changes were fast paced and people had to negotiate a maze. In many ways, each member of the closely-knit society was deeply affected by the actions of others. Their ordinary experiences and stories form the larger history of the people, often untold, which fills in the missing pieces of the people's fragmented history. And so, most of the characters that I've created were inspired by real people and how they dealt with the many changes and challenges in their lives.

During this troubled time of active insurgency in this corner of the country, ordinary people were often living on the edge. The war between the Naga undergrounds and the Indian armed forces often left the common people in a quagmire. During this time, there were certain events that shook the lives of the people. One was the Oinam incident of 1987. The assault and the humiliation of a quiet but proud Assam Rifles camp located at Oinam Hill village in Senapati district of Manipur by the Naga undergrounds one foggy morning escalated into something unprecedented. In an effort to recover the lost arms and ammunitions, the Assam Rifles launched the infamous Operation Bluebird, imposing curfew in about thirty villages surrounding Oinam. The clampdown was heavy on the villagers.

Much of the factual information about the incident is from the book *The Judgment That Never Came: The Army Rule in North East India* (New Delhi: Chicken Neck, 2011) by Nandita Haksar and Sebastian K Hongray. Nandita was the lawyer who filed the original court case against the atrocities of the Assam Rifles, while working closely with the Naga People's Movement for Human Rights and other like-minded human rights organizations. In 2019, close to three decades after the court petitions were filed, Nandita found out, much to her dismay, that the case had been dismissed by the Manipur High Court (the case was transferred from Gauhati High Court) for lack of evidence. It was certainly a shock to her that 'the entire records in twelve volumes running into some thousand pages' were lost. 'Who is responsible for the loss of the brief, the twelve volumes of evidence of large-scale human rights violations of the people of nearly thirty villages in Senapati district?' In a resigned tone she concludes, 'All

I can say, to the people of Oinam and the other villages is that I am ashamed that the courts have not delivered justice and there is no remedy in law against the courts, the judges or the legal system which does not deliver justice...The victims of Operation Bluebird operation will not get justice. Ever.'[1] Amnesty International too brought out a report, which includes many 'eye witness accounts' of Operation Bluebird.[2]

Close on the heels of the conflict between the Naga undergrounds and the Indian armed forces came the bitter and much more unfortunate factional fights that became a greater threat to Naga society. The enemy within has torn the Naga people asunder, leaving many wounded souls. Though concerned citizens call for reconciliation through movements like the Forum for Naga Reconciliation and Naga Mothers' Association, there is still great reluctance to find a common platform. A real solution seems distant. Hatred and thirst for vengeance is written large on the face of each faction and the Christian virtue of forgiveness is far from being practiced in the land where magnificent churches abound. At such a time as this, I remember the lament of the Naga writer Temsula Ao; 'Nagaland's story of the struggle for self-determination started

---

1. Nandita Haksar, 'Manipur Killings, 1987: Charges against Assam Rifles disposed of—though evidence has gone missing', July 16, 2019, https://scroll.in/article/928469/manipur-killings-1987-charges-against-assam-rifles-disposed-of-though-evidence-has-gone-missing

2. For details, see https://www.amnesty.org/en/documents/asa20/017/1990/en/

with high idealism and romantic notions of fervent nationalism, but it somehow got re-written into one of disappointment and disillusionment because it became the very thing it sought to overcome.'[3]

The 'disappointment and disillusionment' is much more when the quest for 'freedom' only brought brokenness and pain to one's own people. When brothers turn against each other, when a village turns against another, I can only see families torn apart and rifts everywhere. I can see many who are deprived of their comforts through no fault of their own and reduced to live lives in extremity. They are like Dickens' Stephen—'It is said that every life has its roses and thorns; there seemed, however, to have been a misadventure or mistake in Stephen's case, whereby somebody else had become possessed of his roses, and he had become possessed of the same somebody's thorns in addition to his own.'[4]

Entangled in all these troubles is the ethnic problem that has splintered the social fabric of many states across the region. Manipur alone has seen several of them play out since the nineties. The Naga-Kuki conflict was immediately succeeded by the Kuki-Paite, the Naga-Meitei and several similar ones that appeared sporadically. The present lull is more apparent and tensions still prevail within. It may be difficult to

---

3. Temsula Ao, 'Lest we forget', T*hese Hills Called Home: Stories from a War Zone, Zubaan*: 2006, p. x.

4. Charles Dickens, *Hard Times*, London: Penguin, 1995, p. 68.

pinpoint the perpetrators of the violence, but certainly the state and other social mechanisms have not been able to contribute to the healing of the wounds that have marred the souls of the people. Often the ethnic divide is so strongly entrenched in the psyche of the people that it becomes difficult to envision a way forward in unison.

While living away from one's own place of birth may seem escapist, because one is certainly in search of a greener pasture, it also provides a bird's eye view of the place of origin. Often, this results in seeing things objectively. For various reasons, there has been a huge outward migration of Northeastern youths from the region, mainly in pursuit of higher education and employment opportunities ushered in by the liberalization process. Yet, they are often reduced to racial stereotypes, often leading to unfortunate events: the Nido Tania case being one.[5] One can say things have improved substantially but there is still a long way to go in addressing the larger issue of discrimination in India.

I hope the stories in this novel find resonance with lives lived in challenging times, wherever, whenever.

---

5. The Bezbaruah Committee instituted by the Ministry of Home Affairs in February 2014 'to look into concerns of the persons hailing from the North-Eastern states who are living in different parts of the country, especially the Metropolitan areas, and to suggest suitable remedial measures which could be taken by the Government.' The report can be accessed at https://mha.gov.in/sites/default/files/ReportOfMPBezbaruahCommittee.PDF

Chapter 1

Three young boys were playing their favourite game of marbles by the roadside. The slanting rays of the sun shone on their faces. Sweat visibly dripped down their foreheads and onto their cheeks, falling to the ground where it merged with the dust. It was just another day in October. The late afternoon was pleasant despite the weather being dry and hot at this time of the year. After all, the rainy season was long gone and the winter not quite in sight. Except for some wandering clouds that played with the sun, the sky was clear and blue. For children, it was the perfect time to enjoy outdoor games. The dusty roadside was their favourite space for their after-school games. Whenever a vehicle passed by, the yellow dust would rise and swirl, disturbing them. But it didn't matter as long as they could get back to their game. They didn't even mind the dust choking them at times. That was like another game. Sometimes, the dust particles seemed to form an image of another playmate.

It was Rakovei's turn, and he had bowled the marbles beyond the line drawn on the ground, which was a couple of yards away. His two friends, Manikho and Kangba, had already identified the target marble he was to shoot. If he could shoot the target marble with his 'lucky' marble he would win the game, and along with it the entire set of marbles. Every kid had his own 'lucky' marble, the best of his collection, which he believed possessed some magical quality. Rakovei's lucky marble was a jet-black one that sparkled when he held it up to the sun. Manikho and Kangba's lucky marbles, which had flowery prints on them, were equally precious to them because they had won many games. The boys cherished this afternoon playtime after school. Their final examination was still six weeks away, and neither their teachers nor their parents were pressuring them to study yet.

But then Rakovei's mother called him. 'Come inside now,' she yelled, 'don't you know what time it is?'

Rakovei hated being interrupted in the middle of a game; after all, he only had a few hours after school when he could play with his friends. Reluctantly he looked up at the sun, which was about to sink into the western hills. But he knew his mother had not called him into the house because nightfall was approaching. In a few moments, the military convoy would be racing down National Highway 39, beside which they were playing. NH 39 was the lifeline of Manipur, as all essential goods for the state came through it. Even at the young age of ten, Rakovei, like all the other children in Manipur, knew the dangers of being out at this time. The neighbour's dog had been run over by one of the notorious army vehicles that routinely zoomed down the highway just before sundown. The memory was still fresh because it had happened just a few days ago. He didn't understand why the convoys were always in a hurry. Were the soldiers afraid of the dark? That is most unlikely, he thought. After all, they were all sturdy men and well armed. Who would have dared to challenge them?

'*Eish*! Is it time already?' he muttered disconsolately, not really expecting an answer from his buddies. They knew that if one of their parents called out to them to return home, the order applied to all.

'All right, last game,' whispered Manikho. And they went on playing.

A few minutes later, each boy reluctantly collected his own set of marbles and went home.

'How many times do I have to tell you to be mindful at this time of the day? Do you think they would even be bothered if they hit you?' demanded his mother when he stepped inside the dimly-lit kitchen. He couldn't understand why his mother always got so agitated when it came to the army. There was nothing Rakovei could say to pacify her. He knew she spoke out of love and concern. Wiping sweat off his forehead and temple with the back of his hand, he sat down on a *mora* in a corner of the kitchen. His straight, trimmed black hair reached his eyebrows. His yellow skin was tanned from walking to and from school in the heat. At close to four feet, he was quite tall for a boy of his age. His faded yellow t-shirt, with the Don Bosco logo and a blue star, was part of last year's school uniform. Now that he had outgrown it, he wore it at home. He wore his favourite pair of checkered shorts and a pair of blue horse-star sandals, one of the many goods that came in from Moreh, the border town at the international boundary which was a well-known entry point for Chinese products.

Rakovei's family's house abutted the road. They had moved to Senapati from their village when he was barely two years old because of his father's job as an upper division clerk at the Deputy Commissioner's office. The town had recently been made the headquarters of the North District of Manipur. Earlier Karong, another town about five kilometres north of NH 39, had been the district headquarters. His father, Khole, a mild-mannered handsome man of medium build, and his mother, Sanei, a beautiful and fair-skinned woman, had bought a small plot of land and started their town life. In the late 1970s and early 1980s, the town was barely a row of houses stretched along the highway, which was also the shopping area. But the town grew over the years as more and more people began to trickle in and settle there, concentrated behind the market line. Sanei started a small store to keep herself busy. She complained that it was boring to stay at home the whole day, being used to working in the fields when she had been in the village. Being from a large family, she had not been able to continue her studies after class V. Since dropping out of school, her main occupation had been to follow her mother to the paddy fields. Marriage and moving to town effectively ended her field activities.

'Mother, can I go and watch the convoy?' asked Rakovei, hearing the sound of the approaching vehicles.

'What is the fun of watching those ugly things?'

There was silence. Though it was almost an everyday thing, Rakovei's mother couldn't understand her son's interest in witnessing the regular passing of the convoy. Nevertheless, she allowed him to go. 'All right, you can look from the front room, but don't step out,' she warned him.

As the convoy zoomed down the highway, with clouds of dust trailing each dark green vehicle, loaded with grim army personnel holding on to their machine guns, the boy's enthusiasm increased. He would count the vehicles each day to see if the number had increased. The roar of the speeding vehicles produced a strange sound, musical to Rakovei's ears. As always, the convoy was in a hurry as though they were afraid of the approaching darkness. Or were they late in reporting for duty? Occasionally, heavily loaded goods trucks would form part of the convoy, even though they would lag behind and try without success to catch up. Yet they too added to the rhythm produced by the military vehicles. Rakovei had a strange fascination with the gang of huge men who never smiled but stared blankly at you with cold eyes. They seemed to be engaged in some serious business. Gripping the heavy SLRs and AK-47s, they looked ready to launch into an offensive at any time. He had watched them at close quarters when they occasionally stopped to buy medicine or other necessities from the nearby shops in the town. And he would marvel at the sight.

Of course, soldiers also patrolled the highway on foot. But they didn't interest Rakovei much because most of them looked sluggish. They lacked the energy and alertness of the soldiers on the vehicles. Perhaps the long-distance travel along the highway took a heavy toll, so that by the time they reached the town they were exhausted. Or perhaps walking around a town was a welcome relief from the forced alertness that was expected of them along the deserted highway. The times were not peaceful. The regular foot soldiers were more vulnerable to wayside ambushes. There was another convoy that would go up the highway towards the north, but since it passed through the town only in the morning, Rakovei usually missed seeing it because of school. The convoys in the late afternoon were the ones to watch out for because the time suited him perfectly. He was greatly drawn to them and marvelled at the way the soldiers never parted with their automatic guns and intimidated even the shopkeepers with their attitude. Or perhaps it was part of their military discipline not to act friendly with strangers they encountered on their way. Rakovei had seen their shin-length black boots, their patterned olive green uniforms, their camouflage suits, and their sturdy helmets at close quarters. Was it the clothes that made the men look tough? He had a deep desire to be like them, to wear their clothes, to wield a gun, and to be 'powerful'.

He didn't know when he began to fancy the soldiers, but that didn't matter. Day after day, week after week, month after month, year after year, he watched the convoy storm down the highway. And his fascination grew all the more. It was a dream he kept to himself. He was rather a shy child and rarely expressed what was on his mind. The first time he had the chance to partially achieve his dream was when his parents decided to reward him for coming first in Class One. When they told him that they would buy him anything of his choice for Christmas, he quickly asked for an army uniform for children. He had seen these tiny uniforms hanging on the sides of shops designed to attract kids like him. Oh, how he had longed to wear one too! His parents were a little baffled at his choice. His mother tried to persuade him to buy a better, warmer set of clothes. But when they realized that he was adamant, they relented. How could they say no to their only child?

Rakovei was thrilled when he got the set of clothes and immediately began dreaming of playing an army officer in search of dacoits with his band of friends. The open space across the highway was their favourite place for enacting scenes they had seen in the movies. They enjoyed pretending to be the good and bad characters. He and his friends often sneaked into the movie halls that had sprung up in different corners of the small town in the past few years. The ticket collector at the entrance would stop them, saying kids were not allowed, but when they handed him a two-rupee note he would let the three of them enter and sit in the front row. Though their necks ached because they were forced to look at the fifteen-inch box fixed right above their head, they nevertheless enjoyed themselves. Unfortunately, they had only finished watching the two-and-half-hour-long Hindi movies a few times because their parents would often come for the next show. On finding them, the angry parents would drag their sons out by the ear. They would feel very bitter, especially when they were forcibly ejected just before the 'last fight' because the ending was always the most intense moment—when the brave hero ultimately triumphed over the bad guys.

The year when he finally got the long-desired military uniform, Rakovei had a terrific time. Clad in his brand-new uniform and with a toy pistol strapped to his right hip, he was an army officer, albeit a small one. His friends offered him the role of the top boss in their games. It was fun to run around, pointing his pistol and shooting the baddies. But now he was older and had outgrown those childish fancies, and was tired of wearing the mock army uniform. Nevertheless, his interest in the army continued, and even grew. He couldn't wait for the day when he would become one of those tough, power-wielding soldiers. Everyone would learn to fear him, he thought.

As Rakovei stood dreamily staring at the street, his mother called out from the kitchen, 'Will you go and bathe? Dinner will be ready soon.' He realized that the convoy had already gone past some time ago. Even the dust that danced to the rhythm of the convoy's passing had settled. The normal quietness of the town had returned. Though the highway was the lifeline of the state, there was very little vehicular movement. Except for the huge goods-laden trucks and the tourist buses travelling to Imphal, the capital of the state, the residents did not see many vehicles. Very few people in the town owned vehicles. Anyway, the town was so small that nobody needed a car. It was this break in the dullness of the town by the military convoy that partly excited Rakovei. It was a treat to watch the army trucks every day, to hear their tremendous roar, and to feel the vibration of the shaking ground under his feet.

Chapter 2

One day in December, at dinner time, Rakovei's father suggested that the family go to Phyamaichi, their native village, for Christmas as it had been a couple of years since their last visit. The little boy was quite excited at the idea. He had been to the village only a few times after the family had moved to the town. He still remembered his last visit when his cousins had welcomed them warmly. They had all had a wonderful time together. He waited impatiently for the days to pass. With the school closed for winter vacation after the final examination, he had nothing to do. And that made the wait seem even longer. He still remembered the long walk to Phyamaichi from Paomata Centre, as there was no bus service to the village. But he was ready for it. Now I'm bigger and taller and can walk for much longer distances, he thought.

Christmas time was always fun, and it was always so much better when they celebrated the festival with friends and relatives in their own village. Everyone knew that town life could be tough during the festivities. People from different communities and religions lived in towns. Towns like Senapati were also home to large numbers of *Lamai*, the term used for people from the mainland of India, who were mainly engaged in mercantile and other essential-goods businesses. They had been living in Senapati ever since the establishment of the township. They had a monopoly over several businesses, including cobbling and barbering. Even though they were not Christians, they celebrated Christmas, but did so in a different way—by making lots of money. Christmas was also a time to buy new clothes. People from the neighbouring villages flocked to Senapati and the usually sleepy town then appeared to be a big city, bursting at the seams with merrymakers and shoppers.

Senapati was the major shopping centre for many villagers in the district. And since the *Lamais* were the main shopkeepers, customers would queue up at their shops during the festive season, when the shops would be open. Richer folks would often head to Imphal or Kohima, or even Dimapur. But for commoners, a visit to the small town of Senapati was a luxury. The town hosted a special day for shoppers called Bazaar Day every Monday. The town committee had set aside a particular open space for the day a little further away from the main town. On that day, traders from different towns, even from faraway Imphal, came loaded with their goods and wares. Naturally, Monday was the busiest day of the week.

Bazaar Day during the winter season always witnessed

a rush, not only because of Christmas but also because people needed to buy winter clothes. They scrambled for second-hand clothes, with jackets, coats, sweaters, and other woolen clothes at the top of their shopping lists. And yet Bazaar Day was much more than just shopping for clothes. People spent money on food that came all the way from the border town of Moreh. Even though these edibles and sweets were available in other small paan shops in Senapati on normal days, the food bought on Monday always seemed to taste better.

That year, Rakovei accompanied his mother to Bazaar Day to shop for various things not only for their own family but also to buy a few gifts for their friends and relatives in the village.

Two days before Christmas, they set out for the village. Rakovei was full of excitement at the prospect of meeting his cousins. He hopped onto the bus, which displayed the sign 'Senapati to Paomata', on its front. But as usual, the bus ride was terrible. They struggled to find a place in the overcrowded bus. People had even clambered on to the roof of the bus. The old and battered bus, crushed under the tremendous weight of passengers and luggage, wheezed along slowly.

'Why don't they provide another bus when so many people travel at this time?' Rakovei complained to his parents, as if they could provide a solution. But all he could do at that moment was complain, knowing fully well that the matter of the overloaded bus was out of their control.

'It's the festive season. Many people are going home to their native places, just like us,' answered his father.

Rakovei knew what his father meant. At other times of the year, he had seen the same bus travel half empty. Sitting on his father's lap, he could smell the horrible body odour of those standing close to him. To make things worse, the bus stopped at almost every village and small town along the highway whenever people waved their hands to get it to halt. At certain places, some passengers got down, mercifully leaving some space for fresh air to sneak in. But the driver kept collecting people to earn the maximum fare. However, nobody complained. Despite the load it carried, the bus somehow sped through the hairpin bends at many points along the way.

After travelling for one and a half hours along NH 39, the bus took the dustier road from Tadubi, the town nearest to the border town of Mao Gate. The condition of the rest of the road was terrible. All those who had dozed off earlier were now shaken awake, and the grind of the vehicle's engine and the kicks of the brake produced a rhythmic sound. The groaning of the overloaded bus became more obvious at this stage. And at times, it would even sulk and refuse to move unless some people disembarked.

The driver stamped on the brake and halted just before a particularly steep area. He shouted from his seat, seemingly to those perched on the roof, 'Get down and give a push!' In a minute, those on the roof and a few other able-bodied men from inside got down.

A few minutes later, the driver called out, 'Okay, everyone push!'

Responding to his call, the ones behind the bus made a 'wohhh' sound in unison as they pushed hard. Rakovei, still on his father's lap inside the bus, found the whole situation funny, as though the vehicle too needed a hand. He thought of the bus as a sulking child who refused to be cheered until his wish was fulfilled. But he also saw that that particular stretch of the road was quite steep. During the rainy season, it was more difficult for vehicles to traverse such terrain because of mudslides, which occurred frequently in this region.

After two hours of the dreary journey, the bus finally reached its destination. However, Rakovei's family still had to walk another three hours to reach Phyamaichi. They were not the only ones covering half of the journey to their village on foot. Getting down at Paomata Centre, they set off without delay. Even though there was a road for vehicles to their village, no public transport was provided. Jeeps for hire were available in Senapati, but not everyone could afford the cost of about Rs. 1500. That was almost half of Khole's monthly income. Naturally, the family did not think of it as an option. Even the little boy knew the family could not afford the expense. He knew that people hired vehicles to go to their villages only in times of emergency. Anyway, he was so happy to go to Phyamaichi that he didn't care what form the journey took. With his small backpack, he moved forward lightly. Even his parents could not keep up with him at first. But a few kilometres later, his tiredness became obvious.

Though the December midday sun would have been comfortable to bask in, the ones making the journey on foot found it hot. They perspired profusely because the sun was directly on them. Only occasionally some wayward clouds gave them a little respite. There were no trees on the particular stretch they were traversing, so they could not even stop to rest under shade. The route passed through Saranamai village, an ancient village which was said to be the ancestor of many villages surrounding it including Phyamaichi. The remnants of an ancient village could be seen, the remains of some monuments dotting the landscape. Stone monoliths stood as symbols of the old. These giant monoliths now seemed to have sprung up naturally, except that they were all arranged in a pattern. According to custom, those who had performed the Feast of Merit would be honoured by a monolith erected in their name. Since this custom was deeply religious in nature, Christianization slowly did away with it.

The hot midday sun forced Rakovei and his family to rest frequently, which they did now on one of the stone slabs beside the huge monoliths. Though they had walked for three quarters of an hour, there was twice the distance still to go. They crossed the Vourei River, a source of the famous Barak River that originated in this part of the region. Terraced fields spread along the stretch of the river. A little later, they crossed the northern boundary of Phyamaichi.

'How much longer will we take to reach the village?' Rakovei asked, just as a way to announce that he was really tired and would prefer some rest. Of course, he knew that there was still a long way to go.

Mother said, 'There is a resting place just a little ahead. Let us rest there a while and have some snacks.' To let sojourners catch their breath and relax, there were several resting places with stone platforms made by the villagers. Approaching one, they rested and refreshed themselves with some drinks and snacks packed from home. They resumed their walk.

'Now you won't be too tired. For the rest of the journey the path will be shaded by tall trees, so we will not be burned by the sun,' his mother said. Sure enough, the boy found it more tolerable walking under the shade of the tall trees despite the clear sky above where the sun was unchallenged by the wandering clouds. An occasional breeze kept their spirits up. The wintry cold had killed most of the greenery in the wooded pathways, but the few remaining clumps of tall grass along the narrow footpath bowed to the travellers as if greeting them. The path was scattered with brown leaves that rustled underneath their feet. Spotting wild chestnuts, the boy bent down to collect them, momentarily forgetting his tiredness. Mother joined him in the search. Who didn't enjoy the taste of roasted chestnuts? They looked like popcorn, but tasted very different. Along the way, they also stopped to refresh themselves with cool water from the streams flowing through small gorges. Though the journey was tiresome and long, the travellers enjoyed the natural beauty of their surroundings.

Now, with more than half their journey behind them, the sun was also slowly making its way into the western sky. The rays of the sun were slanting on them sideways as they progressed on their way. Instinctively, they quickened their pace in order to make it to the village before sundown. Rakovei was tired to the bone, but didn't want to complain. 'Don't worry. We will reach the village in half an hour,' said his father in an encouraging tone. Silently, he endured the fatigue and pushed his legs forward. Soon he was rewarded. He could hear his cousins, Chizüne and Rakho, calling out his name and looked up eagerly, smiling broadly. The children waved at each other. Eleven-year-old Chizüne and eight-year-old Rakho were the older children of Shiveine, Khole's younger sister. They had two younger siblings at home, five-year-old Vahlou and two-year-old Khane. Excited that their cousin was coming home to the village, they did not have the patience to wait at home, and came down to the last resting place before the village to give a helping hand and to welcome the family.

They brought a chilled drink brewed with the local sweet-smelling rice. It was indeed a refreshing drink, which they enjoyed before they finally reached their destination. Chizüne, being a year older, offered to help Rakovei with his backpack. He handed it over with great relief. Somehow, happiness added lightness to his body. As the cousins giggled their way up, within no time they were approaching the village. The sun had dropped into the hills but its rays were still lighting up the horizon. As they passed through the terraced fields, they noticed that some were ploughed while others still awaited the farmers' spades. From a distance they could see smoke curling up through the kitchen roofs of several houses. Some of the thatched houses appeared to be burning, as smoke slipped out from all corners of the kitchen. But this was a common sight, and they were not alarmed. Those who had gone to the fields were seen returning home. A few men with their tools hanging from their shoulders, and some women with their head-strapped baskets, greeted them as they passed by. Despite the simple life revolving around their fields, the villagers look contented and happy.

As soon as they reached the compound, they ran to greet Grandmother in the kitchen. 'Grandmother, look who's come home for Christmas!' Rakovei shrieked.

'Is that you, my boy from the town?' asked Grandmother, turning to see the children storm in through the front door.

'Yes, Grandma. I have come home for Christmas and also to listen to your stories!' he replied.

Grandmother Toukhue was a treasure trove of stories—stories about animals, spirits, people, and all sorts of things about the grand and glorious past. She often tried to teach them songs too, explaining that stories were better remembered when sung. But the kids were not really interested in learning songs. They only wanted to hear her fascinating stories. She would mesmerize them with her way of storytelling, and they could listen till they were too sleepy to stay up. But for that day, the little cousins were too busy catching up after such a long time. As expected, they were all over the place. The shrieks and the shouts that followed them said it all. The joy of reunion brought them memories of the good times they had the last time they were together. The boy from town forgot all the exhaustion of the day's journey and enjoyed the company of his cousins.

Chapter 3

The family house in the village had three bedrooms and a large kitchen. The front compound was large enough for the kids to run around. Most households in the village had a kitchen garden where all sorts of vegetable were grown. Though other vegetables were grown elsewhere, these gardens came to the aid of the kitchen when other stocks had run out. The back door of their family kitchen opened to the garden, and Grandmother picked some fresh mint to add to the smoked beef broth which she had made for the weary travellers.

'Come on in,' she called. 'I've made some light broth for you all. You must be tired and hungry, especially that young grandson of mine.'

The aroma of her broth filled the room. The family exchanged greetings and sat down on the wooden seats out laid for them. 'Dinner will be ready soon, so I didn't make much,' she added apologetically. In the other corner Lounü, Khole's younger brother, was preparing a large chicken for the evening meal.

Grandfather Paosü had died when his children were

young. So Grandmother Toukhue raised their three children, Khole, Shiveine and Lounü, on her own. Since Khole's relocation to the town, the family house had been under the care of his younger brother and his mother. Even though Shiveine was married, she lived just two houses away. And since she would normally leave the kids with Grandmother whenever she needed to do some errands, her family was always around her. Besides, Lounü still being single and Khole's family living in town, Grandmother would often insist that at least one of the grandchildren keep her company on most days. Even though Grandmother would visit Senapati once in a while, she preferred staying in the village. She said the town was too suffocating and noisy for old people like her.

Lounü had come home after graduating from college in Shillong. He had had the chance to teach at the Government High School in the village, but decided not to take it when he learned that the 'opportunity' involved paying money to middlemen. He was very much against getting a job through malpractice, though most people thought it had become inevitable for those wanting a government job. He decided to save his pride and wait for some other opportunity. It shocked everyone, because a government job guaranteed a steady lifelong income. No one really understood his decision. But his temperament was unlike the rest of the family, so no one could really make him consider taking the job. He had made up his mind. He often came to

Senapati town, visiting various offices. One day, he told his brother's family that he had applied for an unemployment loan and was hopeful of getting it. He said he would like to start a small independent business with it. At a time when everyone was vying for a stable government job, he had decided to turn entrepreneur. This didn't make much sense to the other family members who had thought businesses were basically for those who could not secure regular jobs. However, everyone around him respected his sense of judgment and let him be for the time being.

The following morning as the cousins were still asleep, a new day came calling. The chilly December air penetrated their room through the gaps of the wooden planks that made their walls and gently nudged them awake. As usual, the previous evening Chizüne and Rakho had insisted that their parents allow them to stay over with Rakovei at his place. Normally, around this time of year, children stayed tucked inside their blankets even after waking, for it was terribly cold because of the frost. However, the cousins decided not to miss the opportunity of playing in the open. The next day was Christmas, and they wouldn't want to dirty their brand-new Christmas clothes that their parents had bought for them.

As always, with the setting in of the Christmas season, the mood became festive. For the village folks, the post-harvest time till the end of the year was the Christmas season. Since their life revolved around farming, the harvest was a symbol of the fruit of their labour through the year. The remaining one and a half months of the year were, therefore, a time to relax until the dawn of another year called them to begin their activities afresh.

Phyamaichi, with about ninety households, was a medium-sized Naga village. It was only in 1944 that the village was formed, by the first converts to Christianity. Encouraged by the missionaries and ostracized by the larger non-Christian population, which often included members of one's own family, the few who had embraced the new faith moved to settle away from the original village, Phyabu, situated about five kilometres to the east. Over time, it got the status of a revenue village. And more and more people were added to the fold. The population was divided into three main clans, but intermarriages among them made virtually everyone a relative in one way or the other.

As in other places, the missionaries were not just preachers of the Word but also educationists and social campaigners. They set up schools that began with proselytization but eventually attracted even more people. Grandmother said that when they decided to turn to Christianity, it was not so much for the faith that they came and joined the Christian folks in this new village.

'Three of our children died one after the other. And then we heard that if we become Christian we would not face more tragedies, so we decided to come to this village,' she said. Looking back at those years she must have found their way of becoming Christian rather humorous. She continued, 'Initially, we did not really understand all that was preached. We were more concerned about averting death in the family. Strangely, our children born after relocating to this new village are well till today. Of course, our daughter Hrünei passed away, but she was born in the old village and we brought her here as a frail baby. Could it all be mere coincidence? I cannot really say. When I think of those years, I wonder what the reason for all our misfortune could have been. Later, people said that some kind of plague hit the village. And I tend to believe them too, you know, because almost every family lost children. Almost every day we could hear a cry from one household or the other.'

But there could also be the problem of hygiene. Grandmother used to mention how it was difficult to have a clean compound since people shared their compound with cattle and other domesticated animals. And during the rainy season it would really be a mess, she said. If disease broke out, it would be very difficult to control as modern medicine was not widely known to them then. For them, and many others, moving away from the old village and accepting a new faith brought a miracle, practically.

She continued, 'I think many families came to this village to save their children from dying, like us. Whatever it may have been, I'm thankful that we took the decision to move here. Though we left our houses and fields, I have no regrets because my children are alive.'

From the family's compound at the northern end of the village, the view of the church was majestic. Situated on an elevated platform at one end of the village, the church stood above every house. In many ways, the church, built by the first generation of Christians, stood as a symbol of their endeavour. With stones chiseled in equal sizes to make sturdy walls and pillars, wooden tiles of the finest woods from the vast expanse of forest that covered the entire south of the village, it was testimony to the effort of those who truly love the Lord. Although built in the 1960s, it still looked as new as though built only a few years ago.

During Christmas time, it was the tradition to feast together and have social gatherings for two or three evenings. A hall would be made specifically for this purpose at the *dzüdu*, the open space in the middle of the village especially reserved for community activities. Temporary bamboo walls would be erected, encircling the hall to convey a sense of bonding and oneness of the village community. The youth usually made a special contribution in this regard as they not only decorated the Christmas hall to suit the theme of Christmas but also served everyone in other ways. Divided into different groups or houses, they would take turns to cook the community feast and also participated in singing competitions and entertainment during the evening social gatherings. Everyone's involvement in the celebration made it all the more special. The celebrations were a kind of communion, the sharing of a common faith. And the blaring sound of music coming from the Christmas hall would fill the air with happiness. Boney M, ABBA and Jim Reeves had long remained everyone's favourites. They would all be played in turn.

Though the routine never varied, there would be excitement every year. One of the serenities of the start of the Christmas day was the church service. That year, the message of Christmas was brought by the local pastor whose exposition on the theme 'Peace on Earth and Goodwill towards Men' was beautifully done by stressing the purpose of the birth of Jesus Christ. Christmas, the pastor said, was a reminder of God's love for humankind.

Community feasting during Christmas in the village was an essential part of its social life. There would be three or four evenings of feasting, which were usually over before sundown. Following that, huge bonfires would be made inside the hall and different groups would take the stage to entertain the gathering. For the children, there would be no end to the fun of Christmas. Playing around the Christmas hall through the day and enjoying the big pieces of meat served during the feast made them wish that Christmas would come every day!

One evening, the kids decided to stay with Grandmother at home and forgo the social gathering.

It would be a mini celebration of fellowship around the kitchen fireplace, with Grandma entertaining them with her stories. Old age and weakening eyesight kept her from public gatherings, especially the ones after dark. She avoided venturing out after sundown lest she lose her footing.

'Don't worry about me. I will be all right at home alone. You kids can go join your friends and have fun. After all, Christmas celebrations are just for a few days,' she protested.

'It's not that, Grandma,' Chizüne said. 'We want to be with you. It's been a while since we listened to your stories. Please tell us stories.'

'There you go, smart little girl. All right, all right, you win, you naughty ones!' she gave in, a little amused. 'But I don't have new stories to tell. Whatever I have in my memory I must have told you a hundred times.'

'Never mind, Grandma. We can keep listening to you over and over again,' said Rakovei. 'I would like to hear the legend of Pyoupuo Zhio again.'

'Hmm,' Grandmother said as she raked the fire to light up the room. The children looked at her in anticipation. She was silent for a while, as if to recollect the story. Suddenly, as if magically transformed, she looked like one from another life who had come to tell them things they had never heard. Her grey hair turned silvery as the fire began to burn more brightly. The corners of the dark room came alive as if they too wished to listen to her. Everything was silent as she began.

'Long ago, there was a man named Pyoupuo Zhio. He was an extraordinary child from birth and had strange habits. As he grew up, he could often be found hiding in the barn, and would not join the other children of the neighbourhood in their play. He ate only stale food and never ate warm food. Despite the extremely cold weather, he would not sleep on the bed made for him nor put on clothes. As a result, he became very hairy, like an animal. But he was naturally talented in every skill known to man. There was none to match him in wrestling, hunting or warfare. Any hunting party with him in it would always bring the biggest kill. Many tales were told of his legendary feats. It was said that he killed a flying dragon that would swoop down like an eagle to catch its prey. It tormented people for a long time, until Pyoupuo Zhio devised a trap to kill it. It was also said that he killed a giant python that roamed the jungle and would appear from the shadows and swallow a human being in a few seconds. Soon Pyoupuo Zhio's fame travelled far and wide.'

There was a well-timed pause, as Grandmother let the feats of the legend sink in to the young minds. Then she went on, 'Once, a man-eating creature was causing panic in several villages. This monster claimed the lives not only of human beings, but also of domestic animals. People from the villages got together and made concerted efforts to catch the creature, but they were easily thwarted by it. It avoided all the traps set by the villagers and outwitted them in every way. The people became afraid even to go about their normal field work as they didn't know when the creature would strike. Their lives were greatly affected. No one knew what the monster looked like for all those who had encountered it had perished. Some people said it was a two-headed creature who could see both forward and backwards. Other people said it had many limbs with which it could overpower multiple attackers. Yet no one could be certain. But what was certain was that the creature was a wicked and cunning monster.'

The grandchildren, leaning forward and all ears, listened intently to Grandmother's story. They were like three young animals longing to be fed by their master. As the storyteller continued her story with several descriptions, different images of the monster began to form in the imaginations of the children.

Keeping up the momentum, she continued her story. 'One day, representatives of the different villages in the region came to seek Pyoupuo Zhio's help. They described the misery of the people because of the creature. They promised him a suitable reward for killing the creature. Now, it wasn't in the nature of a great hero to decline a challenge, however big or small it may be. He listened carefully to the description of the creature's behaviour and its methods of attack. Then he charted out a plan to defeat his newfound adversary. But he knew this task would not be easy. Not only would he have to prepare himself well but he would also need to equip himself with powerful weapons. After several days of strategizing, he went to the region where the creature had made its home. It took a while for him to locate the hideout. It was a huge, terrible-looking creature. Certainly no mere human being would be a match for it, he thought. Though of human form, it was much bigger and certainly much more powerful. It had a sharp sense of smell, which allowed it to trace human beings. Fortunately for Pyoupuo Zhio, the creature could not smell him because of his food habits. Not having eaten warm food all his life was an advantage for him at that moment. But it dawned on him that perhaps the creature could not be defeated through mere physical strength. It would only be killed through trickery. The other thing that he realized was that the creature was not alone. Though it operated alone outside, it had a family in the hideout, which was a kind of a hole in a cliff. Every time the creature returned home, it would make a certain sound, after which a ladder would be let up for it to descend. Pyoupuo Zhio carefully observed the going and coming of the creature.'

The wonder-struck children's eyes remained transfixed on Grandmother as she continued to tell the story, accompanied by suitable gestures. She was like an illusionist mesmerizing her audience.

'Pyoupuo Zhio practiced the sounds made by the creature till he was confident enough to put himself to the test. One day, after the creature had left for the day's mission, he prepared himself for the battle. A little before it was time for the creature to come home,

Pyoupuo Zhio proceeded to the hole in the cliff and made the sound. Hearing the response from inside, he uttered the second sound. Thinking it was the creature that had come home, the ladder was let up. Quickly, he descended into the hole. Unprepared for an intruder, the entire family was overpowered. Shortly afterwards, the creature came home, unaware of the fate that lay waiting for it. As usual he sounded the first message of arrival to which Pyoupuo Zhio responded, disguised as the female from inside. The creature made the second sound. Then the ladder was let out. As it climbed down, Pyoupuo Zhio speared him on the side, directly piercing the heart. And right there in front of him the ghastly creature took its last breath of life. Pyoupuo Zhio had killed the creature that had terrorized the entire region for so long. With his fine *dao* he chopped off the creature's head to show the people the finest trophy he had won so far and a declaration that the ghastly creature had indeed died. People rejoiced at the victory and honoured him in the most deserving way. That was the legend of Pyoupuo Zhio. He continued to do many legendary feats.'

Grandmother thus finished the story of a legend who lived long ago. But the children sat in silence even though they knew the story had ended. They were still mesmerized by the extraordinary feats of the legend. But they also know that it was Grandmother's art of storytelling that kept them captivated even though they had heard the story several times.

'Tell us another story, please,' pleaded Rakho.

'That's enough for tonight,' said the storyteller.

'No, Grandma. We want to hear another story,' insisted Rakovei. 'Anyway, the social gathering isn't over. And it's a bit too early to sleep.'

The storyteller knew her grandkids had got the better of her. She smiled at them, to say that she would oblige them. She went on to tell them not just one but several stories. And the children listened to her in the most attentive way. It was always a treat to listen to all those stories.

One day, Chizüne asked the storyteller innocently, 'Grandmother, when you're gone, who will tell us stories?' Despite her age the little girl knew that people grow old and die.

'*Hei*, people of this generation don't care about knowing or learning stories that have made us what we are!' said the storyteller sadly. 'Maybe it's their pursuit of modern education that has taken away all their interest in the stories of old. But they do not know that they are more than just stories. They are our history. When we grew up, it was a matter of pride to be able to sing songs and narrate tales. We were encouraged to learn them as it was essential to our way of education. But these days, all you do is read from books and write in them. I don't know what is written in them. Do they tell us about our people? Do they tell you stories like I tell you?'

The girl was taken aback by the outburst. She didn't

know why her grandmother appeared so agitated. Was she expected to answer back? But before she could really understand, the storyteller continued, 'You know, my dear girl, I have seen enough changes in my own lifetime. I don't know if all of them are good. When your parents' generation began to go to schools, every family was excited at the new way of learning. Though not all of my generation was interested in those forms of education, the few who went to school got jobs after a few years. That somewhat interested us. But we didn't know that it would leave them completely disinterested in our songs and stories. I don't know what they did to them at school. I would never know because I don't speak their tongue. They call it the white man's language but it is being taught by a black fellow! There are not many of my generation left now. When the songs and stories die with me, maybe they will regret it, or maybe they won't.'

Grandmother was referring to the teacher from Kerala who had been hired some years ago. Though he was supposed to teach English, due to a shortage of teachers, he would often teach mathematics, science and other subjects too. He was a super teacher with multiple capabilities. His name was Sebastian Mathews, but the village folk couldn't pronounce it and so he came to be popularly known as 'Ja Tei', meaning the black teacher, referring to the colour of his skin.

Chapter 4

The family stayed on in the village till the New Year. It was like an extended Christmas. The few days before the start of the New Year was largely a leisurely time. For those who had wet fields and reared fishes there, it was a kind of ritual to go and catch fish during this time. Winter fish tastes better, they said. The kids were particularly fond of the adventure. It was an adventure for them to step into the ice-cold water in the paddy fields. The chill was exhilarating. These were wet fields where rearing fish after the harvest was considered good. To catch fish, the water would first be let out from a corner of the field. Instinctively, sensing the drying out of the field, the fish would rush and gather into the pond-like area carved out in the middle. Then catching them would be fun!

New Year brought a renewed sense of joy. One of the special attractions of the day was the feasting on *raokhao*, traditional pancakes. They could be made in many different ways—fried in oil, dry-toasted on stone slabs, or cooked wrapped in banana leaves. Sharing too was a tradition. On the first day of the year, young people would go from house to house to taste *raokhao* and to decide who made them the best. With all these traditions, the winter season was the kids' favourite time.

One day after breakfast in one of their casual talks as the children were huddled near the fireplace, Uncle Lounü addressed them. 'So all of you are growing big now...Which class are you in, Rakovei?' Uncle was friendly with everyone. His jovial nature made him every kid's favourite. At almost six feet, he was tall for a Naga. His hair was long and he often wore a cowboy hat. Perhaps it was a way to hide his slightly balding forehead. There was a picture of him with one of those hats and an off-white t-shirt, a pair of tight trousers and a 'Bruce Lee' canvas shoe, which he had framed. The famed Bruce Lee canvas, as it was popularly called then, had a white plastic sole and a covering of soft black cloth. It was a mystery why it was called so, because the flat plastic sole was so slippery that no one would actually do martial arts wearing the shoes. One of his favourite outfits was a pair of unusual faded blue dungarees that he would always wear with a shin-length pair of boots. Since no one wore such distinctive clothes, he was automatically classed apart. Perhaps it was a statement that he lived his life differently.

The kids were all seated together that cold morning. The sunlight hadn't hit their compound yet, so everyone was inside around the kitchen fireplace, trying to beat the winter chilliness.

'I will be in Class V this year,' Rakovei replied.

'That's wonderful,' said Uncle Lounü. 'Rakho here wants to be an IAS officer and Chizüne wants to be a doctor. What do you want to be?'

The question caught the boy by surprise. Secretly he wanted to be an army officer, but he had not shared this with his parents. It was not that his parents were not concerned about his future, but they were not like his uncle, who enjoyed spending time with kids. Rakovei wasn't sure if he should tell the truth or say something else. He turned to his mother, who was on the other side of the fireplace with Aunty Shiveine, not sure if he was asking for his mother's help.

'Umm...I want to become an army officer,' replied Rakovei after pondering the matter for a while. He was imagining the power of uniform and gun that he would like to possess someday. He wasn't prepared for what was about to unfold. From the corner, his mother uttered a '*heigh!*' It was a sound of disbelief, as though something had pierced her soul. Her face dropped and suddenly turned gloomy. Rakovei didn't know what had happened. Only much later did he come to understand. Aware that something was not right, he asked his mother a few days later after they had returned home, if she didn't want him to become an army officer.

'Son, I want you to become anything you want in life except a soldier,' she said with conviction. 'Come here and sit with me. I will tell you a story.'

She sighed. 'I meant to tell you this someday, but I didn't know it had to be so soon.'

Rakovei was bewildered. He wasn't sure what to expect.

'My father died in the custody of the Indian army. I was just about your age then. But I still vividly remember the day they brought his tortured body home.'

Grandfather's name was Voba, meaning pig's stool. Funny as it may sound, that was his real name. During olden times, a newborn child used to be named with bad and unwanted names because it was superstitiously believed that if a child was given a good name, the evil spirits would also want to claim it. Normally, the early death of a child would be a sign that the spirits had claimed it. Therefore, to avert ill-luck in the family, parents would choose ugly names for their children. Grandfather was a noble person, they said. Like others of his generation, he joined the Naga National Council (NNC) as a *vahtamai*, messenger. In the early days of the movement, lots of manpower was required to pass on messages from place to place orally. True to the oral tradition, the messaging system used word of mouth as an effective means of spreading news about the underground movement. Tactically, written communication was best avoided lest the messengers were put in jeopardy. With the movement of the underground heavily checked by the Indian soldiers, the *vahtamai* were the ones who did most of the work, moving from one village to another. Without a requirement for arms, they could move about without suspicion. In a way, they were not part of the underground unit but were common people who engaged in regular activities at other times like any other villagers. Since the beginning of the Naga movement, there were large voluntary recruitments of *vahtamai*. They did not need any modern qualification to be recruited. All that was required of them was to be physically fit as they had to move about incessantly. But since it needed moving from place to place, day or night and could even take days, only men formed this group. In the 1950s and 1960s, the Naga movement grew rapidly. Those were the days when everyone felt obligated to assist or fight for the freedom of the people. In one way or another, everyone was involved, if not physically, then at least in spirit. The times were tense. To most people, it was like the last lap of the struggle to be finally free to determine their own future and not be part of any nation. Unfortunately, the movement became bloodier and deadlier. The unrest continued. The Indian army[6] in trying to quell a small band of rebels, as they initially saw the situation, realized that everyone was part of the movement. Unable to differentiate the underground movement from the rest of

---

6. The people referred to all uniformed Indian armed forces as the 'army'. The distinction between the paramilitary forces and the other military forces was not generally known to the public. And so, to let the spirit of the people seep into the narrative, I've also retained the expression 'army' to mean any Indian armed forces of any uniform, whether it's the Assam Rifles or the CRPF or the IRB or any regiments of any military forces posted in Northeast India.

the people, the Indian military began to launch assaults on the villagers, accusing them of aiding the movement. The result was an ugly turn of events. Villages were burned down, forcing the inhabitants to scatter into the forest or to seek refuge in neighbouring villages. Some villages could not be resettled. Most able-bodied men were tortured because they were accused either of being underground members or sympathizers. The infamous village groupings, or concentration camps, were undertaken to search the villages.

When grandfather Voba fell into the net of the Assam Rifles in 1965, he was not the only one who fell victim to the network of Indian military and their informants. These informants, who were handsomely paid by the army, worked under cover. Their identity was unknown to the public. Their job was to betray the people involved in the underground movement. The army certainly knew that people could be weak when it came to money. Often, certain people were presented to them blind-folded after being arrested by the army to identify the right person. Some believed that these informants were the captured members of the underground imprisoned by the Indian army and coerced into the job under threat of dire consequences if they didn't comply.

It was during one of his messenger errands that the army patrol intercepted Grandfather one evening on an inter-village road. The informant was also in the truck with the army personnel. Grandfather tried to excuse himself, saying he was just visiting a sick relative in the next village. However, luck wasn't with him that day. It wasn't always that an informant travelled with the patrol but that day there was one. He suspected that the informant might have been just taken on board from a neighbouring village. Or there could have been a change of tactic in the army patrol. After all, the creation of the state of Nagaland under the Indian Constitution about two years ago, clearly a move to appease the moderates, infuriated the undergrounds and those in favour of full sovereignty. The Indian army was aware of this difference in opinion among the Nagas. The Nagas soon found themselves helplessly split into different states under the Indian Constitution.

After his captivity, Grandfather was taken to a district jail in Assam where he found many other freedom fighters in custody. When he was released on humanitarian grounds three months after the arrest, he was already half dead. The family was sent word to pick him up from the Assam Rifles camp at Maram. Unsure of how his condition would be, as they had been informed that he had been released on humanitarian grounds, Grandfather's brother and a few other relatives went to bring him home. To the shock of everyone, the state of his health was worse than expected. He was lifted onto the jeep as if a dead body. The soles of his feet had congealed-blood blisters and marks of whipping all over his body. He could never walk again and died three weeks later.

'I never dreamed that I would ever see my father like that,' said Mother, 'so helpless and lifeless. He could not talk intelligibly. He only felt a kind of numbness all the time. Everyone said that was because of the electric shocks. They said that the giving of electric shocks was a regular way of torture to get information about their co-workers. Considering the pain he suffered day after day, I realized that death would have been the better way for him. I was just a child then, but I knew what it meant to hate, and to desire vengeance.'

She paused. Rakovei wasn't sure what was coming next. After a deep breath Mother continued, 'Ever since that time, I hated the Indian army. Every time I see them anywhere, I feel the blood curdling inside me. My son, you must not wish to become an Indian army officer. Don't disappoint me.'

There was nothing the son could say. He could never imagine disappointing his parents who loved him dearly. He now understood the anguish that his mother had regarding the army. But he found it difficult to come to terms with the idea of giving up his first dream in life.

Outside, the sound of the routine convoy rolling down the highway could be heard. Silently he listened to the rhythmic vibration that invaded their house. It must be a new batch of soldiers heading to replace another batch somewhere in the state, he thought. But that day, he didn't move out to watch the convoy. Both mother and son stayed silent for the entire time, waiting for the convoy to pass by. It was like a kind of condolence for Grandfather Voba. Though, in effect, it was the dominating noise outside on the highway that had stifled their talk.

The coldness of the evening began to penetrate the house. January weather was usually chilly. People's habits followed the season. With the sun normally setting by 3:30 p.m., people rushed to prepare their evening meal before dusk. Their action was also necessitated by the erratic supply of electricity. By 6:00 p.m., the streets were deserted. People would hole up inside their own houses rather than risk running into unnecessary trouble with the military forces, who always kept an eye on the movements of the town's people after dark.

Chapter 5

Spring came with all its liveliness. The freshness of the new leaves on the trees demanded a new approach to life. Where life was close to nature, there was more joy. One could watch the hillocks that circled the town change colour this time of the year. The low-lying river below the highway seemed to murmur with happiness and frolic with the foothills beside which it flowed.

But the spring of 1986 brought something unusual. Though a young boy, Rakovei sensed that something was not quite right with Uncle Lounü when he visited them. One day, he overheard the elders conversing about the unemployment loan which Lounü had applied for, which he did not get because of manipulation by a few who had bribed the officer in-charge. Lounü had a graduate degree from NEHU, the North-East Hill University, in Shillong. Most people from the village then did not earn a graduate degree. That he wouldn't be satisfied with a teaching job was obvious. Lounü was ambitious and wanted to hit the big time. He had a business plan, but he didn't have enough capital to kick start his project. That was quite understandable.

Money was the basis of every modern business. After a short stay in the town, Lounü went to the office with his friend Apao to inquire about the loan. As they stepped into the office, the demeanour of the officer-in-charge told them that they weren't welcome. But being in a public office, he could not disallow anybody from entering.

Lounü started, 'Sir, we are here to inquire about the unemployment loan for which we had applied about six months back. Some of those who applied for the same loan have got it, so we would like to know the status of our application.'

The man behind the desk replied, 'If you haven't received any intimation of your selection, isn't it obvious that you have not been picked?'

'But, sir, we have applied for the same loan,' said Apao. 'Why is there favouritism?'

'How dare you question my authority?' demanded the officer. 'If you wanted yours to be selected, you should have done the same thing as those who have received the loan.'

Lounü was quick to get the hint. Corruption had deeply corroded society with those in positions of power making hoards of money in dishonest ways. So, this is what it has come to, he thought. He wasn't a person to be intimidated easily. The next moment he did the unexpected. He grabbed the wooden chair that he was sitting on and hammered the officer who could barely shield himself from the blow. Thankfully the injury was not fatal. Anyway, Lounü wouldn't have wanted to murder somebody. Perhaps he thought the injury was enough to teach him a lesson. The officer had become notorious for manipulating the system, many people said. Afterwards, he calmly walked out of the office and his friend trotted behind him. Apao was petrified by what he just observed, but Lounü didn't show any remorse.

He coolly stepped into his brother's house, packed his bag, and told his sister-in-law, 'I have to leave now. Please tell brother that I had to rush.'

'Why? What happened?' she asked, alarmed at the urgency. Her husband wasn't back yet from office. Lounü narrated his story and left for the village.

Khole came home, soon after his wife told him of what had happened over the phone. He became restless.

'What the heck!' he cried. 'Does he think that he can get away after committing such a grievous act? He doesn't know what trouble he has got everyone into!'

'It's too late to change the situation now,' said his wife, not too sure if it would placate him. But she continued in a saner tone, 'It's best that we tell him to be cautious for now and tell him not to come here till the situation gets better.'

Apao later visited the family to see if they were all right. He felt obligated to explain things to his friend's brother's family. He said, 'I couldn't believe he didn't show any fear after committing the act. He didn't even look back to see if somebody was pursuing him. He just walked out calmly as though he hadn't done anything, despite the pandemonium in the office. Man, he had the heart of a lion!' He was still nervous as he said those words.

'I think it would be wise for you too to stay low for now, rather than just walk around,' Khole advised.

'That's right,' he said, suddenly conscious that he could also be arrested as an accomplice for abetting the act. So far, he hadn't thought about himself. He was too consumed with thinking about what could happen to his friend. He quietly and hurriedly left for his house, which was situated on the outskirts of the town.

As expected, the next day's newspaper carried a report of the assault on a government officer with the department in which the officer worked strongly condemning it. But there was also something unexpected. First, a couple of the newspapers misreported the incident and turned the whole episode into a communal one, because the officer was a Meitei, from the valley-based community. This was totally blown out of proportion. The valley–hill animosity was becoming obvious lately and everyone tended to read any petty incident involving different communities in the state that way. Did Lounü manhandle the officer because he was a Meitei? Would he have done the same if the officer were a Naga like him? Nobody knew. But there was speculation. Secondly, a search and arrest warrant was ordered and the 21 Assam Rifles was assigned to carry out the order. That was quite ironic. The police was supposed to keep law and order, but the more powerful army was called in immediately. On what pretext was the warrant issued? Nobody dared to question it. The Assam Rifles went into action to find the guilty person.

Knowing that the armed forces could reach the village any day, word was sent to Lounü to leave Phyamaichi and seek refuge in a neighbouring village. He set off to the next village where he stayed for a few months at a relative's house. Somehow the dream of starting a business also began to fade. Though he came back to his own village after a few months, he couldn't really stay on, because the men in uniform would routinely come searching for him. But the family in the village realized that the armed forces were in pursuit of a person they could not identify as they did not have his photo. They realized this when the armed forces first came to look for him and, after ransacking the whole house, finally asked for a photo. Thankfully, the family had hidden away virtually everything that belonged to Lounü. Taking a clue from this, and realizing that a change of identity would be helpful, Lounü changed his name to Lenny. Thus, he became Lenny for the rest of his life.

Life wasn't the same anymore. Lenny couldn't really live his life even in his own home. That frustrated him. The Assam Rifles kept coming in search of the fugitive at regular intervals. But normally their arrival would be known much before they reached the village. They only came on foot and anybody out in the fields could announce their approach. So Lenny was often home, after the initial few months, without tension. However, one day the armed forces stepped into the compound unannounced. And as fate would have it, Lenny was taking a nap inside. Only his mother was around with her two grandchildren, Shiveine's two older kids, that day.

Her heart began to pound the moment she saw the uniformed men with guns stepping into their compound. Though she had dreaded the day of arrest, she definitely didn't want it to be in front of her eyes. She said a silent prayer as she stepped out to face them. At the sight of the soldiers, the two kids clung to the legs of their grandmother. They were shivering and on the verge of crying. The leader of the searching band smiled at them, but that didn't change the situation. Grandmother told them to go inside the kitchen, and they went. The midday sun was scorching hot outside and the men in uniform asked for water to drink, speaking in Hindi, but simultaneously making the action of drinking. Having served them, Grandmother made a sign that she didn't know how to speak their language.

'Is anybody home?' the leader asked, regardless of her action.

Again Grandmother made a sign, nodding her head. But she made another sign telling them to wait, and went inside. She wasn't sure if she was doing the right thing. But certainly, she thought, it would be much better to tell her son of the soldiers' arrival herself rather than let him be abruptly woken by the soldiers, which would obviously shock him.

'The army is here,' she said in a manner as composed as possible so as not to frighten him. She clearly wasn't sure how her son would take it. He woke up, alarmed, but tried not to panic.

'Yeah? What have you told them?' he asked, getting up slowly. For once he didn't know how to face the adversary.

'Nothing yet. I barely know how to communicate. I just made some signs to wait outside.'

There was no back door for him to escape through. But even if there was, flight would only put him in danger. What should he do now? Could this be the end of the road for the fugitive? As he walked slowly out from his room to face the army, he thought hard. Then an idea struck him. Perhaps he could fake his innocence. After all, hadn't he changed his name? As he stepped out on to the veranda, the lethargic group of uniformed men outside suddenly became alert.

The leader of the army asked, 'Are you Lounü?' He was unable to pronounce the name right, the 'ü' somehow turning into a rounded 'o'.

'No. My name is Lenny. I'm a relative from the next village and have come here to help my aunt chop some firewood for the coming winter season.'

The lieutenant looked at him intently, not sure if he should believe this young man. Meanwhile, that day the Village Authority was holding its meeting in one of the neighbour's houses and Grandmother had sent Chizüne, the older of the two kids, from the back door of the kitchen to inform the people at the meeting.

'Is he not your son Lounü?' the lieutenant asked Grandmother.

Again, Grandmother acted ignorant. But she told her son in their own tongue, 'The Village Authority's meeting is being held at Yu-o's house. You had better ask for help.'

'What did she say?' inquired the army leader, a bit startled at the conversation in the native tongue.

'Oh! She only said there's a meeting of elders in the house over there and you could verify my identity from them,' answered Lenny, not too sure if he had said the right thing.

'All right,' said the lieutenant and sent a man to tell one of them to come out.

Lenny became suddenly concerned. Of course, everyone in the village knew that it had been some time since he had changed his name and somehow everyone had got used to his new name. But what if the fellow summoned unwittingly identified him as Lounü? No, no, that couldn't happen, he said to himself. Just then an elderly fellow stepped into the compound with the soldier.

'Who is this man?' the lieutenant asked the elderly man, not giving him a chance to say anything first. The look on Grandmother's face indicated that she was feeling weak. Her son tried his best not to show any sign of distress.

'He's Lenny,' said the elder. What a relief that was for both mother and son standing in the veranda. But the lieutenant wasn't convinced.

'Are you sure this is not Lounü?' he enquired.

'No, sir. He's just a relative of the family from the next village visiting them.'

The lieutenant and his band of eight soldiers uniformly cursed their ill-luck. Fatigue had once again returned to grip them. When they thought the hunt had come to an end, the apparent identity of the person before them had thrown them back into the search operation. They would have to keep looking, under the scorching heat of the sun or drenched in the rain. But that day, they were not in a position to make their journey back to the camp. They asked for directions to the community hall where they normally spent the night if they had to stay in the village on an operation.

'Phew! What luck!' said Lenny, as soon as the army was out of sight. He sat down on the cane chair on the veranda, trying to defuse the tension inside him.

'Don't make it sound funny!' Grandmother said. 'You don't know how much heartache you have given me. What do you think I would have felt if they had arrested you today?' She was still emotional and partly angry too. 'Don't call it luck! It was God who saved you today. At least, for my sake. The Lord knows I would have died if they had taken you.'

Lenny didn't know what to say. Yes, it was true. His mother loved him more than she loved her other two children. Perhaps he was more notorious and temperamental so that she had had to be more mindful of him since childhood. 'Either he will bring me happiness or he will take the life out of me,' she would often say. Since he had become a wanted man, she grumbled often about his decision to not take the teaching job when he had the chance.

'All this is happening because you refused to heed my advice. You should have taken the teaching job when you had the chance. Now you cannot even dream of it.'

'Oh, come on, not that again, *pfü*,' he complained. 'Why do you keep mentioning it when you know it wasn't the right way to get a job?'

'But everyone's doing it that way!' she said. Bribery had become commonplace now.

'Just because everyone's doing it, it doesn't become right,' he corrected. 'What is the worth of my education if I can get a job only through bribery? In any case, where would we get the money?'

'If you had agreed, we would have found a way. And if you had taken it, by now you would have been comfortably settled with a family of your own. And you wouldn't have landed in this trouble.' After a pause she added, 'Look at me, I'm growing older by the day.'

He could sense the urgency in his mother's voice. After all, like all parents, she wanted to see her children settled well before she grew too old and surely before her death. But he wasn't a person who would be content with a teaching job for the rest of his life. He didn't know how to react but he said, 'Mother, you don't have to be that emotional.'

'Why not? Look at people of your age group, they're all married and have kids. You're twenty-eight already. I would love to see my grandchildren from you, but I don't know if that will happen. My death may come before your marriage.'

'You don't have to compare me with others. Many of them are school dropouts and eloped at a young age.'

'*Hei!* In my generation, men got married by twenty-two, twenty-three. Now you are trying to say that education has delayed your settling down in life.' She paused for a few seconds and began, 'My son, I did not send you to pursue education to delay your marriage. There's a right time for everything. The more you delay your marriage, the harder it will be for you to find a girl to marry.'

That was food for thought, Lenny thought to himself. It's not that he was running away from jobs, he had just not found something he wanted. He had been seeing a girl and he knew about the pressure to commit from her side too. But then, how could he settle down without finding a source of income? He had been banking on the unemployment loan to start something on his own. But that had been busted, too. For now, he was just a fugitive running for cover. How long would it take until they gave up? He was living an uncertain life at the moment, paying for an impulsive mistake. He had not foreseen how greatly it would affect his life. All he could do at that point of time was to wait till the armed forces became distracted by a new turn of events, strong enough to draw their attention away from him. He was an optimist at heart and hoped things would soon change.

Chapter 6

1987. A new year. For village folk the dawn of another year meant starting afresh their annual activities. January was still extremely cold in this part of the world. Besides, the village was located at the foothills of Khyouchi, one of the highest hills in the region, with a wide expanse of forest close to it, which made it colder. The evergreen forest was home to many wild animals and birds and also produced the finest woods, including *vaosü*, the king of woods, and *chahsü*, a native oak-like flowering tree, both of which were much sought after as timber, and considered excellent material for wooden houses. All the houses in the village were made of wood sourced from the forest itself. Though aluminium and tin roofs had lately become the preferred option as they lasted longer, there were still a lot of thatched houses. And though the tin houses looked modern, the thatched ones gave a more homely feel, and even the swallows made their nests in these cozy thatched houses.

The main occupation of the village folks had long been rice cultivation. Other agricultural activities abounded, but it was the paddy fields that demanded the most attention. Traditionally, there were two main forms of paddy cultivation, the slash and burn or *jhum* cultivation and the wet or terrace cultivation. Since Phyamaichi was located in the foothills where water was abundant, most people preferred wet cultivation. Wet cultivation itself was of two types, one that used water throughout the year, with fish rearing taking place post-harvest; and tilled cultivation which took place at the end of the harvest and after which the lands remained fallow. But the villagers grew other crops as well. The land being fertile, practically every form of agricultural activity was productive. The first two months of the year were spent tilling the paddy fields and on identifying locations for other crops. For school children, every new session began with excitement. The winter season was long enough for these young ones to forget the tediousness of school life.

Spring was everyone's favourite season. By the third month of the year, the seed-planting began. The rains would follow soon and were welcomed. The trees and plants sprouted new leaves. The freshness of the season would be accompanied by warmth, the winter having passed and the summer not yet set in. Children liked to take full advantage of this season. Since the school day ended at two in the afternoon, they had ample time to play around in the warmth of the day. Unfortunately, the season of good times didn't last long for them. Because by the time the rainy season set in, there was no real chance to play outside. When it rained, it rained a lot. Sometimes it drizzled for days too. Though the sun would come up, the continuous days of rain usually left the ground soggy and muddy. The children could not play outdoors. At such times, their games were limited to the kitchen where the fireplace would keep them warm. It was a different kind of fun, enjoying popcorn and roasted pumpkin seeds.

'Tomorrow is *shithaine*. We also want to help with the transplantation of paddy in the fields!' declared Rakho, beaming. His parents didn't like to disappoint him. The boy was referring to the first day of paddy transplantation. Community life was regulated, and the village folks would set aside a day for this activity. No individual family was allowed to transplant paddy in the fields before this day on their own. It was observed with a sense of religious sacredness since it marked the beginning of the transplantation season. On the eve of the day, a celebration was held where wrestling competitions among different age groups would be performed with pomp and show.

'Why don't you wait till the school is closed for summer vacation?' said his father.

HIs mother turned to see the suddenly saddened face of her son. 'Let them come, if it doesn't rain. After all, *shithaine* comes just once a year,' she said, feeling sorry for her disappointed son. Rakho's face immediately lit up.

The sun rose early the next day, as if to grant the

children their wish. As promised, they followed their parents into the fields.

Two weeks later, the school was closed for summer vacation. The kids were happy because they would be able to join their parents whenever they wanted. The transplantation season was usually the busiest two months of the year for the villagers. Despite the incessant rain they couldn't afford to rest. With their plastic sheets shielding them from rain, they continued their work. Here and there you could still find a few people wearing their hand-woven rain shields made of wild bamboo. But more and more people had begun to opt for the cheaper and easily available colourful plastic sheets. Though a very tedious job, paddy transplantation was an essential task for the traditionally rice-dependent people.

The village folks had evolved a unique system of rewarding themselves after their hard work, from the seed sowing to celebrating the completion of transplantation to the post-harvest celebration. After the successful completion of the paddy transplantation, they celebrated *Laonüh*. Traditionally, the festival had been celebrated for a week, beginning at the end of June until the first week of July. But now only a couple of days were set aside for the festival.

Deeply religious in nature, these festivities were to give thanks to the spirits for granting a suitable climate for the successful completion of their work. The festival continued to be celebrated despite the fact that most village people had converted to Christianity. Interestingly, people had appropriated the religious significance of the festival by attributing all thanks to the Christian god. Perhaps the transition was made easier as they had only to give the name Jehovah to the previously unnamed benevolent god in their belief system.

At their Senapati home, Rakovei begged his parents to let him join his cousins in the village for *Laonüh*. 'You keep promising me every year that you will let me go 'next' year, but this year I'm not buying that excuse,' he protested. 'I heard that Aunty Duchaoe has come to town with two of her colleagues for some church work and they are leaving the day after. Please speak to them to let me join them, *pfü*. Look, I'm twelve years old now and I can carry my own stuff without anyone's help.'

Mother used to make excuses that he was not big enough yet to travel without one of them. That was a fair reason. And the boy knew that Mother could not leave Father alone as it would be too much for him to handle both office work and household chores. The last time his family was in the village during *Laonüh* was about six years ago, and he barely had any memory of it. Every year, Grandmother and his cousins would send him *todjo*, traditional food items of the festival, through someone or the other. That would heighten the boy's excitement and also his disappointment at missing the festival for another year. Mother knew this well, and she also knew that her son had reached a sensitive age.

It would hurt him more if they were to make the same excuse of him being too young.

After a while, Mother said, 'OK, let Father come back from office. I'll talk to him.'

'I don't think *apuo* will say 'no' if you're willing,' the son said. The summer break would go on till the end of next week, so he was hopeful that he would be allowed to go. They all knew that coming back wouldn't be a problem as many older students who stayed on for the festival would hurry back after it and Rakovei could join them. Later that evening, he was elated that his parents allowed him to go to the village for *Laonüh*. But they also had an ulterior motive. They had been trying to coax Grandmother to visit them, but she wouldn't come. It had been more than a year since they had last met. And with age catching up with her, Grandmother had become more resistant to travelling. Hopefully, her grandson's coming would please her enough that she would drop him back to Senapati herself.

Two days later, Rakovei hopped on to the bus in great excitement. The young boy dreamed the whole time in the bus, imagining how excited his cousins would be to see him come home for the festival. He could barely remember the festival. As usual, the bus ride ended at Paomata Centre, and the journey on foot began. Halfway through, it began to rain. However, he couldn't complain. After all, it was the rainy season. The wind accompanying the rain drenched him all over despite the umbrella. He looked across at those accompanying him and found they were also in the same situation. But sooner than expected, the travellers reached the village. A day later, the much-awaited festival began.

The sun rose early to greet the *Laonüh* festival, bringing cheer to everyone. Traditional dances and songs formed the main attractions of the day. And of course, in the true spirit of the Nagas, lavish feasting on meat was a key element of the festival.

'*Pfü, puo*...can we also join our friends later for the feast?' Chizüne and Rakho requested their parents at the morning meal. Before the parents could say anything, the older girl added, 'This is the first time for Rakovei and he's so excited about it.' The girl was confident that she had given them a reason they could not refuse.

Different age groups were allowed to feast together on this day. Now that the *morung* system of separate dormitories for boys and girls of different age groups had been replaced by the day school, young people took advantage of the festival to feast among themselves. Young as they might be, the kids were in the mood to be faithful to the festival tradition.

'What would you do? None of you or your friends know how to cook!' replied her mother.

'Maraine knows how to cook,' responded Chizüne, referring to one of her friends at whose house they proposed to feast together.

'Hmm...how sure are you of that? We don't want you to have ill-cooked meat.'

'Oh! It will be all fine,' said Rakho, not too sure if that was the best way to assure his parents.

Mother was able to have a word with Maraine's parents to let the kids bring along home-cooked food. Towards evening when the kids came home their parents told them that they would be allowed to join their friends on the condition that they eat only home-cooked food. Other parents had also been asked to do the same, they said. Though a bit disappointed, the kids realized that this was much better than not being allowed to go to the party. Joyfully they packed their tiffins and headed towards their designated location. Innocent as they were, they derived happiness out of the simple things in life.

The next day was just another day of relaxation at home for most of the village folks, except for a few who needed to look after their cattle lest they stray into the fields. As usual, after a good season of transplantation they deserved some time to recoup their health, because after a while it would be time for the season of weeding. A couple of men who were out for some necessary work in the fields sighted a band of Indian soldiers approaching their village. Though they were used to the visits of soldiers from time to time, especially after the search for Lenny had begun, this time they were alarmed. First, they seemed larger in number than the usual patrolling unit that came looking for Lenny, and secondly, they were coming from a different direction. Since there had been no prior information, one of the villagers said, 'This doesn't look right. We should inform our folks. If they have come for Lenny, we should tell him, lest he be caught unaware.' With that they headed home, half running.

True to the suspicion of the two men who first sighted them, that day the soldiers of the Assam Rifles had come for a different operation and it didn't seem friendly from the start. The villagers knew this immediately when they beheld the stern faces of the soldiers marching into the village. The contingent was led by a major. Without wasting time, the major summoned the Lokho, the village headman, and ordered him to supply chickens, rice and other essentials to feed the newly arrived troops. That didn't surprise him, as those were the usual demands on their visits. But the more distressing news was that a curfew was imposed on the village. One of the Village Authority members stood on the *chukho*, the raised stone platform in the middle of the village where men's meetings were held and announcements made.

Clearing his throat, the man announced, 'This is for everyone, whether at home or out in the fields. Please listen attentively. Just a while ago, a big group of army personnel arrived in our village. We have not been properly informed of their purpose as yet, but they have imposed curfew in our village. Movement after sundown has been restricted, and so everyone is requested to stay indoors. No one shall be allowed to travel. Let this be taken as a serious matter. Anybody found violating this order shall be deemed responsible for his or her own action. If there is anyone out in the fields or in the forest, you are requested to hurry home immediately. Further announcements shall be made as and when necessary.' He turned to the other side of the village and repeated the announcement.

The message was received with a heavy heart by everyone. No one understood why. But pretty soon the word got around through the grapevine that this was the counter-operation of the assault on the Assam Rifles post at Oinam Hill village by the NSCN, the National Socialist Council of Nagaland, the previous day. The situation suddenly became tense. Everyone was gripped with fear. Nobody knew what the army was up to. Between Phyamaichi and Oinam there was just one village and only a small mountain range separated the two. News didn't get across so quickly in the villages because there was no telephone. The village did not even have electricity.

A group of young boys playing football abruptly stopped. They all looked upset. Everyone was clueless as to what the announcement meant. Since the playground was at the far end of the village, they didn't see the arrival of the Assam Rifles. Only when they were headed home did they realize the ominous situation that had gripped the village.

Back at home, three-year-old Khane, Shiveine's youngest child, snuggled against his mother's bosom. A familiar fear had gripped her too. 'Have the soldiers come to take me?' she asked. 'No, dear. They won't,' her mother assured her, a little amused. Being the youngest she demanded attention all the time and would cry often. To stop her from crying, her mother would often scare her by saying that the soldiers would come for the children who cried. Such warnings were enough to make children stop crying instantly. Mothers often used this strategy to deal with crying children. The soldiers with guns had always been a symbol of fear in this part of the region, rather than of security.

Mother and daughter stood on their veranda. Shiveine anxiously looked towards where her son Rakho and Rakovei had gone to shoot birds. Earlier during the day, Rakovei had ventured out with his cousin who was a year younger but far naughtier. He was very excited that he could stay for a few more days in the village. With a catapult each and sling bags loaded with clay pellets, they went to the nearby forest. Rakho was an expert in the art of shooting birds and a master in rolling the clay pellets perfectly into the size of marbles. Though just eleven years of age, his accuracy with the catapult had always produced results, allowing him to bring home some birds for the evening curry. That day, too, the boys thought they were lucky to have shot some birds. But they didn't know what awaited them at home.

After half an hour of waiting, Shiveine could see the boys appear in the distance. They were half leaping and half walking with excitement. 'Didn't you hear the announcement?' she scolded them the moment they stepped into the compound. The boys weren't expecting to be welcomed home with a scolding. Rakho raised his voice, 'We did.'

'Then why didn't you hurry home?'

They had no answer. They stood silently, with bowed head. The older cousin's shyness had turned into embarrassment. He hadn't expected a day of fun to end like this. But the younger cousin stood firm, perhaps a show of strength since he had endured such admonishments in the past. Just a while ago, they had been ready to show off their catch of the day, three big birds. But Rakho's mother's outburst suddenly restrained them. As Shiveine made way for them, they silently walked into the kitchen and placed the birds on the cupboard. Quietly they grabbed a wooden seat each and moved towards the fireplace to warm themselves. Chizüne was helping her mother in the kitchen. 'A large group of army soldiers had come to the village,' she whispered to the boys.

'We heard that. But what's the big fuss?' Rakho asked. The sight of the soldiers had become a regular thing, especially since Uncle Lenny had become a fugitive.

'I don't know for sure yet, but I overheard mother and father talking that some undergrounds had attacked an army camp.'

July 9, 1987. It was just a normal day at Oinam Hill village. With the paddy transplantation over, the villagers were looking forward to another day of relaxation as they waited for *Laonüh* which would be held in a few days' time. The celebration of *Laonüh* varied from village to village by a few days depending on the completion of transplantation. Since it had rained the previous day, the early morning was a bit misty and cold. As early risers raked up their fireplaces, smoke could be seen coming from the kitchens and merging with the mist. Soon the sun began to shine on compounds. But the next few minutes disturbed their tranquility. They heard gun shots from the Assam Rifles post located at the northern end of the village, about two hundred yards from the last house.

'Were those gun shots?' queried one of the village headman's neighbours. Both of them, like the others, had ran out of their houses to figure out what they had just heard. Before the headman could respond, they heard shouts and cries coming from the army camp. And then more gun shots.

The Assam Rifles military post at Oinam Hill village was set up in the mid-1960s. It was also around this time that the first ceasefire between the Government of India and the Naga National Council (NNC) was brokered by the Peace Mission consisting of Bimal Prasad Chaliha, Rev. Michael Scot, and Jaya Prakash Narayan. Though situated in the North District of Manipur (present-day Senapati District), the whole Naga-populated area was under the influence of the Naga national movement. Oinam Hill village was located on a hilltop, and the army post occupied a strategic vantage point as it overlooked many neighbouring villages. Over a period of time, it had become a full-fledged military post, with the families of soldiers staying there and with a proper canteen in place. Though they kept their distance during the early days, the soldiers soon established friendly relations with the villagers and they began to engage in mutual help. The soldiers would seek assistance whenever they required essential commodities like vegetables, firewood and meat.

Likewise, the villagers could use the canteen at the army post, purchasing goods at rates cheaper than those in the market. Besides, they didn't need to go the distance on foot for many essential commodities. The nearest town was Maram and it was a good day's journey to go there and back. At other times, the youth would even engage in some friendly volleyball games inside the camp. But a single day's incident changed all that.

On that fateful day, everyone in the army post was caught off guard. The sentry somehow did not notice the adversary slip inside their camp. Did the NSCN cadres glide inside with the morning mist? Did they turn into spirits so that they became invisible to the soldiers on duty? No one could tell. But what was certain was that they came well prepared and acted swiftly. The precision of their action showed that they had most likely surveyed the camp before the attack. They entered the camp and shot down almost a dozen of those who were armed, including two junior commissioned officers (JCOs), and injuring some of those who tried to retaliate. The swiftness of the operation didn't offer the soldiers a chance to wire an SOS message to the nearest military post at Maram town, which was ten kilometres away. The rest of the unarmed soldiers and other non-combatants like the cooks and the families were ordered into the mess hall and locked in by the invading Naga army. Next, the NSCN army went straight to the armoury and carried away all the weapons and ammunition in store. They took the help of the able-bodied men of Oinam to carry the looted weapons into the jungle.

Panicky and uncertain of their fate, those who were locked inside the mess hall huddled together. Was this how it would end for them, unarmed and humiliated? How rewarding it is for those who have died in action, they thought. Mixed feelings of anger and self-loathing rose in their hearts. But as they were preparing to die, the camp became eerily silent. Had the underground Naga army left without killing them, their enemy? What adversary would leave their foe alive in an attack? It took some time for them to realize that the NSCN cadres had indeed left. They peeked out to ascertain the situation. Then one of them sneaked out of the window and broke the lock of the main door. One by one, they came out, still gripped by fear. Seeing the bodies of their fallen comrades, many of them began to cry. Some were dumbfounded and didn't know if they should cry for the tragedy or laugh because they had gained a second chance at life. Others were yet to recover from the shock.

Why didn't the NSCN cadres kill all their adversaries? Was it not the Indian army that had driven them underground? Did they forget that they had locked up the rest of the soldiers and their families in the mess hall? Or had they intended to spare them? Perhaps they were not there to kill everybody. Their mission that day was to loot the weapons, and not kill people as far as possible. With their operation successful, they left in the same way they had come—without a trace. The weapons snatched by the underground NSCN from the Assam Rifles post at Oinam Hill village were to go down in history as India's biggest weapons cache lost in a raid since the start of the Indo-Naga conflict. But the price of the victory of the NSCN was paid heavily by the innocent people of the village and several other villages surrounding Oinam Hill village. The retribution of the Assam Rifles for the humiliation suffered at the hands of the Naga underground was far beyond imagination. The military post at Oinam Hill village was closed down and never reopened. Perhaps the suspicion that the villagers had joined hands with the undergrounds to bring down the military post ran too deep for them to rebuild the trust.

But the villagers were as ignorant as the Assam Rifles about the plans of the NSCN. On the day of the incident, the villagers too were rudely awakened to the shocking attack. Perhaps the plan had been strictly limited within the undergrounds, for fear of leaks. Yet no matter how precisely the plan was executed, the NSCN certainly underestimated the resurgent spirit of the Assam Rifles and the extent to which they would go in seeking vengeance. For all they had done, the undergrounds were mute with horror at the actions undertaken by the Indian soldiers. Why didn't they come forward and defend the people whose freedom they claimed they were fighting for? They took away the weapons and never spoke a word. And the innocent people suffered for their sake. Was that how it was planned, to make the people the scapegoats? Surely they miscalculated the retaliatory might of the Assam Rifles.

The raid at the military post only lasted a few hours. By midday the army choppers were flying in. Soldiers were sent in and the injured were air-lifted by helicopter to their main base at Maram. Simultaneously, a convoy was seen speeding up the road, with huge clouds of dust trailing each vehicle. The Oinam post was packed away in a hurry. Without losing time, the Assam Rifles launched its counter-operation on the pretext of recovering the lost weapons and ammunition. They were well organized, and a contingent headed by a commanding officer was sent to each of the thirty villages around Oinam Hill village. They hoped that the underground Naga army had not got too far with the arms, and if speedy action was taken they might recover them. Thus they launched the infamous Operation Bluebird under the direct command of Major General P.L. Kukrety, General Officer in Command of the recently created 'M' (Manipur) sector based at Maram (earlier it had been under the command of the army base at Jakhama, Nagaland) with the full backing of Lt. Gen. K.V. Krishna Rao, the Governor of the state. In an astonishing revelation a year later, Brigadier B.N. Singh, DIG of Assam Rifles, admitted that the Assam Rifles was assisted by a number of other Indian military forces during Operation Bluebird, including the 61 Infantry Brigade, the 59 Mountain Brigade, the 81 Mountain Brigade and one battalion of the BSF, among others.

For more than three months, from July to October, the villagers in all the targeted villages were cordoned off by the Assam Rifles in their search operation. With curfew imposed, movements were restricted. Public transport services were stopped. The villages in the entire region were cut off from the outside world. Military rule was enforced stringently. They not only wielded power over the people in the villages, but any civil authority that tried to enter these villages was severely reprimanded or beaten up.

For all that time, Senapati District was virtually under siege by the Assam Rifles. Neither the Deputy Commissioner nor the Sub-Divisional Officer and the Sub-Divisional Collector of the area nor the Superintendent of Police were allowed any access to the areas affected. All the complaints, allegations and letters seeking clarification were dismissed by the military as false. The sitting MLA of the constituency, Shri Benjamin Banee, who happened to be from Oinam Hill village, was even picked up by the Assam Rifles and harassed. The chief minister of the state, Reishang Keishing, a Tangkhul Naga, wrote a letter to the union home minister informing him about the excesses committed by the Assam Rifles and requested his intervention since the Assam Rifles, being a paramilitary force, came directly under the Ministry of Home Affairs. Though the home minister did visit the state in September, he did not visit the affected district, much to the disappointment of everyone who had been protesting against the atrocities of the Assam Rifles. Various human rights organizations in the state had been protesting against the highhandedness of the Assam Rifles and the Armed Forces Special Powers Act. The All Naga Students' Association of Manipur demanded a judicial inquiry into the torture and killings by the armed forces. The Goodwill Mission Team members of the Naga Students' Federation were prevented from visiting the villages. Instead they were arrested and tortured. The Naga Peoples Movement for Human Rights actively condemned the brutalities of the Assam Rifles and waged legal battles in the courts for a long time.

Chapter 7

The day following the arrival of the Assam Rifles contingent at Phyamaichi, the villagers awoke with anxiety. No one was sure about the situation. The sun rose as usual and the clear sky promised a pleasant day ahead. The chickens and other domestic animals were up and about. But the village was unusually quiet because the people were in a subdued mood. The second announcement of the previous day from the Village Authority had warned people not to venture out to their fields or to travel lest they be caught in unnecessary trouble. The soldiers had positioned themselves at all strategic locations to oversee people's movement. As the new day began, a most unwelcome announcement was made. Everyone was ordered to vacate their houses immediately after the morning meal and proceed to the church. Anyone found disobeying the order would be punished severely, the people were told. Besides, they were told not to lock their houses.

The contingent of soldiers had occupied the community hall and the Lower Primary School which was just below it. Both the LP school and Junior High

School were closed without notice. The pastor's quarters, located opposite the community hall, was ordered to be opened in order to accommodate the leader of the army, Major R. Singh. Since the pastor at that time was from the village, he chose to stay in his own house and so the pastor's quarters were only used as a guesthouse for any visiting missionaries. On special consideration and after observation, three physically challenged persons were allowed to stay at home with someone to take care of their needs. This was done after the Village Authority begged hard on their behalf.

Soon after everyone moved into the church it was locked from outside and two soldiers were stationed as guards. A few of them were stationed at strategic locations, overseeing entry and exit points of the village. Since the village was located on a hillock, it was easier to mark the way in and out. The rest of the soldiers were sent to search inside each house. Split into two groups, each group was sent to either end of the village to begin. Most of the people were still clueless about the Assam Rifles' action. Of course, the Village Authority had been told and through them the word spread secretly. But as the villagers were restricted in their movements, the grapevine wasn't a very effective means of communication. Only inside the church did the rest of the people come to know that the army was on a search operation for the arms and ammunition looted from the Oinam camp by the NSCN. They clearly thought that the underground cadres could not have carried the weapons far. However, the villagers had a different reasoning and were deeply annoyed at the way things were unfolding. Why would the Naga army hide arms in villages rather than shipping them to their camps? Did the Indian armed forces fear that the NSCN planned to arm the villages to fight against India? Or was it just an excuse to vent their anger because of the NSCN assault?

The soldiers on duty went about their search operation, kicking open weak doors and knocking down barns, perhaps thinking that the looted arms were buried inside. House to house, the two groups went about their task, but it was a fruitless endeavour. And their anger increased, partly because of their failure. Meanwhile, the villagers inside the church were losing patience. Since the time they had entered the church, no one was allowed to go out, even to answer nature's call. The children were restless and cranky. The chairman and the secretary of the Village Authority who were summoned to the major's makeshift office pleaded with him to release their people, but to no avail.

Thankfully, the search operation in the village came to a halt by midday. When they were expecting relief for everyone, the news came that only women and children would be allowed to leave. Men had to stay for questioning. However, they could go out to answer nature's call in the church premises, but had to be back inside the church in ten minutes. Nobody knew what would come next. One by one, women and children filed out of the church under the strict surveillance of the soldiers who stood with their fingers hooked on the trigger of their AK-47s, ready to fire at anyone who made an unusual move.

Those freed from the church reached their homes only to find them ransacked. The domestic animals and birds had found their way inside the houses and had eaten their fill. People wept on seeing the mess left by the searching soldiers. As most people were mourning the terrible conditions at their own homes, a woman raised an alarm.

'Oh! Look, people, the cattle have wandered onto some fields at *müzhe*!'

Many people had their paddy fields there and on hearing the alarming announcement they ran out of their home to look towards *müzhe*. Though far away, this was the patch of land which could be seen directly by most people whose houses were in the northern part of the village. Because of the curfew, nobody could go and redirect the cattle elsewhere, as in normal times.

'Oh mother, oh father, what will happen now!' cried Shiveine's neighbour. She was one of those who went out to look towards *müzhe*. 'As if knocking down my granaries was not enough, now the cattle have run amok into my fields! Now what do my family live on? Oh God, have mercy!'

One after the other, those who had fields at *müzhe* began to sigh and weep. Anxiety gripped everyone. They all had fields somewhere or the other. What guarantee was there that cattle wouldn't wander into their fields? Anger and sorrow filled the village.

Animals are animals. They do not have sense like human beings. If only *müzhe* was close enough for the villagers to chase the cattle away. Anger and sorrow filled the village.

Young Rakovei was teary with fear as he sat down with his grandmother who was overcome with worry. If only I hadn't come to the village for *Laonüh* this year, thought the boy. But then how could he have known things would turn out this way? All good times were short lived. In a few days' time he was supposed to head back to Senapati with Grandmother, who had agreed to go. Now, everything looked uncertain. He sorely missed his parents. The last time he remembered feeling so scared was four years ago when curfew had been imposed in Senapati town because the NSCN had gunned down a plain-clothed captain of the military intelligence of the Assam Rifles in front of a tea hotel in broad daylight. Only a few shots were heard. With the job neatly done, the killers sped across the river and disappeared into the forest. The reaction of the Assam Rifles came very late. Curfew was imposed to allow the soldiers to search every corner of the town. Did they think that the undergrounds would be hiding in town after the shootout? Even though a few witnesses told the soldiers that they had seen the culprits escape across the river, they still continued the search. Perhaps it was for their own satisfaction that they carried out the operation. Coincidentally, at that time too, grandson and grandmother had been caught together in the curfew. The little boy held onto his grandmother, who was on one of her visits. After that she swore she would never visit Senapati again. But soon she forgot about it and visited the town two years later. She came down for her grandson's sake.

But this time, things were much worse. And Grandmother was unusually apprehensive. Her grandson sensed her anxiety as she did not pay much attention to him despite him being fretful.

Finally, she spoke, 'I hope Lenny will behave in front of the soldiers. He's very temperamental, that uncle of yours. I have always been worried about him. He's so unlike the rest of us. I don't know where he got that heart of a lion. And after he became a wanted man, my heart has weakened terribly. I fear I will die someday hearing some bad news about him. Oh, God, be merciful...'

The boy wiped his tears and felt a deep sympathy for his grandmother. But he wasn't sure how to console her, so he sat quietly.

Meanwhile, the men were brought before the major to be questioned. The major's ruthlessness and terrorizing attitude had earned him the title 'Tiger Major' among the people. Besides, some could not pronounce his name, so the easier nickname became popular. At the interrogation, some faked ignorance of Hindi, the language in which they were being queried, thereby being sent off quickly. The more informed and educated men and those in positions of influence were questioned first. To start with, Lokho, the chairman of the Village Authority, was manhandled, slapped and hit with rifle butts for requesting the major repeatedly to release the people held inside the church. However, Shekho, the secretary, defended himself by producing his certificate that proved him to be a member of the now defunct Village Voluntary Force (VVF). But he too was not spared the verbal abuse, even from the low-ranking soldiers.

When Joseph, the headmaster of the Junior High School, was called in, he was asked to provide information about the families in the village whose members belonged to the NSCN. The major spoke in English, perhaps as a way to encourage the headmaster to confide in him. But after a few rounds of questions and no satisfactory answers, the major got angry with him. Where there are greater expectations, the failure to live up to them invokes more anger.

'You are a man of great respect in your society because you are the headmaster of the school,' Tiger Major said. 'If you assist me in getting the information that I want, I have the power to set you free. Understand that. I will give you a chance today and let you go, but do not expect me to spare you tomorrow.'

The six-foot-tall leader of the military contingent stood up, revealing his imposing physical stature as he issued the warning. He was like an angry tiger about to pounce on its prey.

The headmaster left without saying anything. For the sake of his people, he hadn't said anything or passed on any information. But the next day, again, the same curfew would be imposed. That much he could infer from the words of Tiger Major.

Then Houba, a sixty-two-year-old man, was produced before the major. He was straightaway asked, 'So how long has your son been in the UG?' The frail man felt the first bite; his strength drained away. After all, he thought, they had information about his son. Should he tell them the truth? Or should he fake ignorance? Either way, he was trapped. He weakly answered, 'It's been a long time, sir.'

'Today, you'll have to pay for not preventing your son from fighting against the nation. Wasn't he part of the ambush team that looted the arms and killed our men at Oinam camp?' asked Tiger Major.

It was a rhetorical question and the major wasn't expecting a reply. He ordered Houba to be whipped. The army regularly tortured family members of the UGs as a way of avenging the assaults they had suffered. They forced Houba to lie down on a bench and a soldier whipped the soles of his feet with a cane. He yelped with pain. The people inside the church were alarmed by the shouts of pain. They grew angry. But the cries continued as the whipping now proceeded up his body. He couldn't stand on his feet when he was ordered out. The penalty for having a son in the UG was a lifelong chronic infirmity.

When it was Lenny's turn, half of the men had already been questioned and had been sent home. Except for Houba and a couple of others, no grievous injury had been inflicted. With no members of his family in the underground, he was confident that he would be let out quickly like many others. But as he stepped in, he felt it wasn't all well inside. Tiger Major was seated near the window and the light coming through it somehow concealed his true appearance since the room inside was not lit. Outside, the sun was slanting towards the western sky. Some papers lay on the table at which the major was seated.

'Tell me about your family,' he said.

'My father died when I was small. I don't have many memories of him. My brother works as a UDC in the DC's office in Senapati where his family lives. I have a sister who is married and lives in the village. My mother and I live here in the village.'

'What do you do? I hear you have a bachelor's degree.'

He didn't know how to answer the question. He couldn't see where all this was leading. Early this morning, his mother had woken up a bit disturbed and said she had had a bad dream about him. And she warned him to be careful. 'Do not be impulsive,' she said.

'So far I have only been looking for employment, sir.'

The smart and witty major continued with his interrogation. 'An educated unemployed youth.

Are you a member of the UG? I hear they're now recruiting people like you. Or are you one of those working overground and passing on information to the militants?'

A few years ago, soon after his graduation, his childhood friend Daniel had tried to persuade him to join the UG. Daniel was now married to his cousin Rakhune and they had a son and another child on the way. With the marriage, the two friends had become even closer despite the physical distance that separated them. Ever since he had dropped out from school, Daniel had been with the UG. The last time he had visited Lenny, he really pressed his friend to work for the 'nation'. 'We need educated people like you more now since the breakup,' he stressed. He was referring to the formation of NSCN in 1980 by those who condemned the Shillong Accord of 1975. With A.Z. Phizo, the father of Naga nationalism, silently holed up in England and conspicuously silent on the accord, those who were back home became restless. A few years later, Isak Chishi Swu, Th. Muivah, and S.S. Khaplang formed the NSCN. They promised to carry the torch of Naga nationalism forward.

But as the major threw those questions at him, something stirred inside him. The word 'militant' didn't quite ring right in Lenny's ear. To everyone the undergrounds were the 'national workers' fighting for the freedom of their people who believed they had been forcibly made part of India.

'They're not militants, sir,' he stated bluntly.

'Ah! So here's somebody who has the guts to declare what he feels!' cried the major, provoked at this defence of the undergrounds. 'How are they not militants when they kill soldiers who defend the nation? They attack our camps and ambush those on patrol...Tell me, what are they?'

It was now obvious that the army leader was only looking for an excuse to punish the young man in front of him.

Lenny was in a fix about how to answer. To defend the undergrounds would land him in further trouble. But not to answer was no less a defiance. He decided to reaffirm what he believed and said, 'They are our "freedom fighters".'

Incensed by this answer, Tiger Major growled, 'You bloody rascal!' and gestured to the soldiers to take action. Before Lenny could react, the butt of a rifle hit him on his right temple, knocking him senseless. The second rifle butt landed between his ribs and spinal cord. Within seconds he fell with a 'thud' to the ground and lost consciousness.

When he came to his senses, he found himself at home, on a bed in the living room. He had a throbbing headache and his back was burning with pain. He could hear his mother and sister sobbing in a corner. Some neighbours attended to his needs and talked in whispers. Two lanterns on either side of the room provided light. Outside, it was already pitch dark and the sound of the wind blowing against the tall bamboos in the garden could be heard. It sounded like the gnashing of teeth.

His brother-in-law, Veikhainü, was dressing his head wounds. 'How are you feeling? Will you be able to sit up to have some food?' he asked.

He was famished, but pain and soreness had quelled his hunger. He had bled profusely from a cut on his temple, but their neighbour Veinü, a self-taught physician and doctor to the whole village, had dressed it. Even though the village had grown sizably, there was no medical facility available for the villagers. There was a small government dispensary in the neighbouring village, but the curfew prevented anyone going there.

The next day, the headmaster of the government junior high school was severely tortured along with a couple of others. The village remained anxious. Besides, their concerns over the newly transplanted paddy fields had heightened since most of them could not be seen from the village. The wayward cattle could have destroyed them or water might not be flowing in properly as it had not rained for a couple of days. But there was nothing they could do.

A few days later, a highly unwelcome bit of news spread in the village. The army major had asked for a tall and beautiful girl named Hraveine whom he must have seen when the army had rounded up the entire village population. The girl cried with fear and her parents called the womenfolk to physically guard her even at night with sickles, and be ready to defend her in case the soldiers came for her. (Somehow, the womenfolk believed that the soldiers were scared of the curved sickle.) Knowing that the villagers would not give in to such an outrageous demand, the major tried to play down the whole drama as a mere rumour, but the people did not believe this and continued to be protective of their women, ensuring that they were always in groups and never ventured out alone.

It was only much later that they came to know that the army came down heavily on those villages which were reported to have more prominent members in the UG. Phyamaichi was one such village. Fortunately, no one was killed as a result of the torture as had happened in some villages closer to Oinam. Between Phyamaichi and Oinam stood Purul village. Perhaps this geographical distance protected Phyamaichi. Besides, the route which the NSCN army took did not pass through the forest of Phyamaichi. Even so, enough harm was done to the people in the village. Lenny, Houba and Joseph, the school headmaster, were grievously injured while a few others endured various forms of physical abuse.

Meanwhile, in other villages, the same tactics were adopted by the military forces, curfew and search operations, except that torture was not carried out in all the villages. But Oinam and the villages nearest to it bore the brunt of the army atrocities. Within a few days of the attack on the Assam Rifles camp, many deaths were reported. The first casualty was a sixty-five-year-old woman who died of trauma seeing the harsh measures meted out to her fellow villagers by the armed forces. Many youths admitted to helping the UGs in carrying arms and ammunition to the jungle, but told the soldiers that they did not know anything beyond this. The youths involved were whipped with iron rods, hit with rifle butts, and some of them were suspended on poles for hours. The chairman and the secretary of the Village Authority were arrested and their families were not informed of their whereabouts. A couple of days later, the people of Khungdei, a neighbouring village, found the bodies of these men with marks of torture on the road that led to their village. Perhaps they had been taken to show the escape route that the undergrounds took, but were killed for non-cooperation. Khungdei village lay to the south of Oinam and the route that the Naga army took was via the thick forest that surrounded the village. It also had some prominent leaders in the underground. Another leader of the village died of extreme electric shock. Many others were bound and whipped with rods, and chilli powder was rubbed on their genitals.

Women in many villages suffered physical molestation at the hands of the soldiers. They were left to defend their houses when the men were tortured. Many of them saw their loved ones beaten and abused. There was blatant violation of human rights everywhere. One of the most shameful and barbaric acts was when a woman was forced to give birth in full view of the villagers and the soldiers at Oinam Hill village. This incident occurred exactly a week after the launch of Operation Bluebird. It took place during one of those search operations where people were forced out in the open. Despite the incessant rain, the villagers were forced to stay out on the playground that separated the village and the recently abandoned Assam Rifles camp. The husband of the woman and the members of the Village Authority pleaded with the commanding officer, Lt. Col. C.P. Sharma, who was leading the operation that day, to be merciful and allow the woman to rest at home as she could give birth any day. But their pleadings fell on deaf ears. As fate would have it, she went into labour while still out in the open. Was it the weather that hastened the labour? No one could say. As the day progressed, the woman's labour began to increase. Once again her husband along with the Village Authority members went to beg the CO, who was seated comfortably in a safe corner under a tent, but again they were abused and sent back. Knowing there was no way of reasoning with the army who was out to get revenge, they retreated to join the people at the open ground.

Thankfully, sometime later the hard rain stopped, but it continued to drizzle. The ground was already filled with muddy water. Tormented children huddled with their parents. The women, joined in their sisterhood of pain, shielded the woman in labour from public view. She screamed in pain as her baby forced its way out.

On the side her husband and other relatives wept at the critical situation. After a while, the cry of the child was heard. But the ground was filled with blood and muddy water. So far, people had seen only animals give birth out in the open, but that day they witnessed a human being reduced to the status of an animal. But human beings were not used to animal conditions. The baby certainly didn't expect that the world would be so cruel. To suddenly face the chill of the naked world straight from the warmth of the womb was too much for the baby. The newly born child died a few hours later.

Chapter 8

Early one morning in mid-August, Khole and Sanei rushed to the village in a hired Mahindra jeep to pick Lenny up and take him for medical examination at the Regional Institute of Medical Sciences in Imphal. Rakovei had missed classes for almost three weeks now. When they heard of the severity of the torture by the Assam Rifles on Lenny and others in the village, Khole sought permission from the Deputy Commissioner to go and take his brother to the hospital for treatment, but the administrative head of the district too was stripped of his power by the Assam Rifles, and so nothing could be done. After many days of insistence, the DC finally granted a letter permitting them to undertake their journey, citing urgency. Besides, word had spread that the operation and the curfew had been somewhat relaxed in certain villages which were a bit removed from Oinam Hill village.

As they entered the room where Lenny was lying, they sobbed openly. Lenny's temple had a deep cut and the wound was still raw. After some time, Shiveine came and called them to have some food. After her children had eaten their morning meal, she had come over to help in the kitchen at her mother's house.

'We were stopped several times on the way,' said Khole. 'Even though we had the letter of permission from the DC, we were interrogated every time. We had to pull out the paper every time and answer all the questions. We would have reached earlier if not for these unnecessary delays.' His voice was agitated. And his anger had risen after seeing the grievousness of his brother's injuries. Lifting his head and turning towards his sister, he asked, 'How is brother-in-law coping?'

'He's ok. So far, he has not been manhandled. But his older brother was hit twice with a rifle butt on the back and now complains of breathing problems.' After a little pause she continued, 'You must have heard of Uncle Houba. He's in a terrible state, and I heard a few days back that he's coughing blood. And the same thing happened with Joseph, the headmaster. He, too, was severely beaten, and has been lying in bed, unable to move.'

'How did things come to this with Lenny?' inquired Sanei.

'Nobody knows what exactly happened inside. I don't know what provoked the soldiers to torture him this badly,' responded Shiveine. 'I tried to ask him once, but he wouldn't answer. After that I didn't want to press him. You know how he is.'

Khole joined in, 'Do you think the army knew of his association with Daniel?' Before anybody could answer, he added, 'But how would they know? In any case, he hasn't gone to join them.' He was referring to Daniel's insistence that Lenny should join the NSCN. The family knew all about it. In fact, Grandmother had been very upset with Daniel because of this incident. Since the army had been after him, Lenny had even contemplated joining the underground, at least to escape the constant searches. However, Grandmother was dead against it, and he knew it well. He wouldn't want to bring more heartache to his mother.

Turning to his mother Khole said, '*Pfü*, I think we should leave soon.'

'Leave today itself? I thought we would be leaving tomorrow morning. I am not ready. Won't we have problems on the way if it's late?'

'It shouldn't be. We've got the paper from the DC. The earlier, the better for Lenny. I don't think the district hospital at Senapati can help. We'll have to take him to RIMS in Imphal.'

For once, Rakovei was also eager to leave the village. Earlier, he was always keen to leave Senapati and reluctant to leave the village after the holidays. But not this time. However, he didn't want to show his eagerness to his cousins. It would send the wrong message, he thought. After all, he was leaving them at an uncertain time. Saying bye, he sat down by his grandmother. For once, he felt very sorry for his cousins in the village.

'Shiveine, don't forget to feed the chickens,' cried

Grandmother. 'There is some grain as well as some corn in the *sülai,* the wild bamboo basket, behind the kitchen door. And a load of pig's fodder is kept on the ground beneath the water storage tank.' Grandmother had always been fond of rearing chickens. However, of late, she had stopped keeping as many as before. Now she preferred to rear a small piglet, hoping to sell it once it became too big for her to feed.

'Don't worry. I'll take care of things here,' answered her daughter.

Lenny was helped onto a wooden plank over which a mattress was laid. He had complained of back pain since the torture. He had tried to sit up a few times, but couldn't sit for long, so for most of the time he lay on his back or turned to the side. He had lost a considerable amount of weight within a few weeks as he wasn't eating well. Considering that the rugged road would cause trouble for his back, he was moved into the jeep on the wooden plank that was to be his makeshift bed throughout the journey.

At the road exiting the village, the soldiers on sentry duty stopped the car to check it thoroughly and asked how everyone was related to the man lying on the wooden plank. For the first time, a deep sense of anger grew in Rakovei at the men in uniform. Seeing them at very close quarters, he realized there was nothing admirable about their looks. They just looked dangerous, with their automatic rifles in their hands. Under the midday sun they smelled horrible.

Their body odour was worse than the people in the crowded bus, he thought. And then, looking at his uncle, now immobilized because of them, a fresh anger sprouted inside him. Somehow, something changed in him that day.

The journey was slow, as they had to be careful of jolts that would hurt Lenny. An hour later they crossed the border of their village lands. The sun had begun to slant down. But the road till the Vourei River was a bit slippery, so the ride was relatively fast. At the point where the road branched towards Oinam, a major military check-post was set up. Sand-filled gunny bags were piled up to make two sentry posts, with one soldier each holding automatic machine guns pointing in both directions along the road. They had to stop there and explain the urgency of the trip.

'They knew we were the same people they had stopped earlier. Why do they have to question us again!' complained Khole.

'Let them be, Khole. It won't be good to get tangled in a fight,' his wife said, trying to pacify him.

They were stopped three more times on the NH 39 till they finally reached Senapati. Though it wasn't sunset, the rain clouds hovering in the sky had shielded the sun, signaling rain by nightfall or the next day. The town doesn't feel right, thought Rakovei. He could see more soldiers on the road. Two checkpoints with piles of mud-filled bags reaching chest height had come up at both ends of the highway. They appeared to be stationed comfortably as though they had always been there. What he didn't know then was that the Assam Rifles had usurped power from the civil administration of the district since Operation Bluebird.

As they sat down to have tea after the tiresome and long drive from the village to the town, the sound of the military convoy coming down the highway vibrated through the rooms of their house. The noise stifled the soft conversation of the family. They waited silently for the convoy to pass.

The following day, Mother woke up her son and informed him that he had to go to school. Uneasily, he got up. After his morning meal, he was putting on his uniform when his neighbour called out to ask if he was ready. 'Almost,' he said. It's good to have friends who are always there, he thought.

'We're going to Imphal to take your uncle to the hospital. And we're not sure if we will be back today, but Grandmother will be at home with you, all right?' Mother said.

'Okay,' he answered. Even though he was a young boy, he had grown sensible to the needs of the hour. 'But has *apuo* filled the leave page in my progress report?'

'I already have,' shouted Father from the washroom, 'and I've also attached a leave application explaining the reason. Don't worry, everyone knows about it.'

'Really? Did everyone really know what was going on in the village? Did they know about my uncle?' he wondered. With these thoughts still on his mind, he went to the table and found his father's application. Going into the room where Uncle Lenny lay, he stared at his uncle in deep thought. Then he went back, picked up his school bag and went to join his friend waiting for him outside. On the way, his friend asked him about the situation in the village. Rakovei was surprised that his friend also knew. At school too, the teacher called him over during the recess and asked him about the people in the village and his uncle. He had to tell her what he had experienced. Suddenly everybody seemed to know. But then, how could they not know? His absence for two weeks after the summer vacation was enough to make them curious. It was only later that he came to know how the ripples caused by the army operations in several Poumai villages had been felt even at the headquarters of the district.

Chapter 9

That evening his parents called to say that they wouldn't be coming back because Uncle Lenny's treatment was not complete. That left Rakovei to deal with his grandmother's anxiety about her son. But he didn't know how to soothe her worries. He tried to divert her by telling her stories about his friends, his school and so on. Still, the conversation would lead to Uncle Lenny. After a while, thinking he would let his grandmother do the talking, he asked, 'When were you born, Grandma?'

'Oh, don't ask me such things. People in those days did not consider it important to keep a record of births and deaths. We were born, that was it. Nowadays, people keep a track of when they were born and celebrate birthdays. But I guess when we were born, people had too many things to do so they forgot to celebrate birthdays!' She laughed at that.

'But your parents must have told you of a period or some season when you were born, no? Perhaps some of your friends who are still alive have some clue?' probed the boy, trying to make her remember. For once, he thought he had found a topic that would engage her.

Grandmother was such a fine storyteller that she would talk non-stop once she got going. He was happy to hear her.

'Yes, they did,' the old woman said. The boy leaned forward to hear her story.

'My parents told me I was born right after the Great War that was fought in some very distant land. They were able to say that because some of our people were also recruited by the white people to help them.' She paused, as though to remember if she had missed something. She was referring to the First World War when many able-bodied Naga men had been recruited to serve in the British Labour Corps. Stories of their experiences were told for generations after they left. People marvelled at their stories. Some just wanted to know of the world outside. Then she went on, 'I must have been born towards the end of October or early November because they said it was post-harvest and the weather was favourable. I don't remember any extraordinary incidents when I was young. But then another big war came. I remember distinctly the plight of the Japanese soldiers.' This time she was referring to the Second World War when the Japanese went through their land while marching towards Kohima, the stronghold of the British in the Naga Hills.

'Wow! You encountered them?' interrupted her excited grandson. Instantly, his interest increased. 'Tell me about it!'

'Well, I was already married by then. Sadly, we

had lost our first child. When we heard of the war, we thought it was too far away for our world to be involved. Anyway, it wasn't our war. But when the Japanese soldiers came trooping into our land, we knew the war was very close.'

The Imphal–Kohima War, fought in the middle of 1944, was the worst large-scale war witnessed by the people of the region. It was then that they realized what modern warfare did to human beings. When the Japanese soldiers entered the remote hills, they had successfully defeated Imphal and were marching towards the other major base at Kohima. But penetrating the rugged hills took a toll on them. Most people of Grandmother's generation weren't initially sure if the Japanese had lost their way or if they were intentionally following a route when they crossed their village. They looked weary and lost, Grandmother said. But their numbers said they were following a route. Everyone was scared because they had guns and no one spoke to them. But some leaders overcame their fear and tried to talk to them by way of sign language. With much difficulty, some time later, they learned that the soldiers had come via the Tangkhul country. Then they pulled out some money, signaling that they wanted to buy food. They did so by pointing at the dried maize hanging on the porches of some houses and the vegetables growing in the gardens. It was the beginning of April and since the rainy season had begun, they were all wet. They managed to communicate that they had run out of rations.

'It was strange that they looked so much like us, except that their language sounded funny. Out of sympathy, we offered whatever food we could. From what I heard later, they pulled out a map of the region and asked those speaking to them to direct them towards Kohima. By then everyone knew there was a war going on. But it was a pity to see many of them very sickly. We knew many of them would not make it to their destination.'

'Did they come back the same way?'

'I don't remember. Given the condition they were in, I worried they would not be able to take another step,' she said. 'But many days later, some hunters came across their tracks and found some dead bodies, barely covered in shallow graves. They said they were scared to touch the corpses for fear of communicable diseases. But it was not a surprise because we knew they would not make it far. It was much later that we heard of similar stories from people travelling to other Naga areas.'

'Do you think they were all killed in the war?' asked her curious grandson.

'*Hei!* How would I know everything, my grandson?' she answered, rather amused. But she added that the loud noise of bombing could be heard and that they figured out that the explosions were taking place in the Angami and Chakhesang areas. Kohima wasn't too far away. Sometimes aircraft could also be seen flying above them. Only much later did they learn that the villages around Kohima had been bombed heavily. The old motorable road, which later became NH 39, was the main route taken by the Japanese as they marched towards Kohima. At Mao Gate and in some of the surrounding villages, the Japanese took shelter to regroup before they finally resumed their march to Kohima.

She took a short break to recollect her thoughts and began again after a deep breath. 'When you asked about them returning the same way,' she said hesitantly, as though she wasn't sure if she should continue, 'there are stories that many of them retreated from the battle at Kohima. But it seems many were not able to join the retreating army or those who had surrendered. Nevertheless, they were not many in number and many were wounded, people said.'

'Really? What happened to them?' cried Rakovei, excited at the sudden twist in the story.

'They became part of us,' Grandmother calmly said. This sounded surreal to the boy.

'What?' he asked, not sure if he had heard her right.

'It may sound absurd, but it's true.'

'But how?'

Grandmother thought for a while, a bit unsure about how best to tell this part of the story. She was searching for the right words. The boy looked at his grandmother, breathing slowly so as not to interrupt the story in any way. Then she began, 'My grandson, there are times when a society chooses to let things lie silent. And everybody respects it. That is the reason why the stories of the Japanese soldiers who were adopted into Naga families ceased to be told.'

The boy wasn't sure what his grandmother was saying. But to clear the confusion in the mind of the young boy, the storyteller added, 'When the Japanese soldiers ran away to escape death, they sought shelter in the nearby villages. Many of them were wounded, as I told you. Now, it is not in our Naga culture to harm someone, even if he were our adversary, if they come seeking protection. In any case, the Japanese were not our enemy. And they hadn't done us any harm that we should ill-treat them. When these soldiers ran to the villages for cover, it was said they were pleading, that they were in tears. The villagers felt pity and treated them well. The wounded were also treated and in due course they recovered. But days passed and they didn't show any sign of leaving. It is not in our culture for a host to chase away his guests. So they stayed on for a long time. They didn't show any sign of wanting to go back to their country. Soon word spread that there were more of them in other villages too. And that they had become friendly, eating whatever we ate. So some villages decided to adopt them. After all, they looked like us, they said. Slowly, the Japanese soldiers learned our language. Surely they knew they had come too far to go back on their own. It is said they were soon adopted into the clans willing to take them in. Over a period of time, they married and had kids.'

'Is that really possible?' cried the grandson. 'I mean,

in our tradition?' The boy had yet to understand all the cultural nuances of his own people.

'Well, it has always been thus,' answered Grandmother. 'That has been our culture from ancient times. You see, sometimes that's a way of providing refuge to a person who may have committed some offence in his own village, but has run away to another village. There are laws of the land that banish an offender, even though that person may have committed the offence as a result of oversight. Our culture rarely permits penalty by death. And so whenever the offender seeks the protection of another village, he promises to abide by the law of that land and to bear good conduct. In turn, the host village vouches for his safety and the willing clan and family adopts the new member and his family, if applicable. That is our culture, and everyone respects it. After the completion of the years of banishment, he would be given the choice of returning to his original village. But if he is willing to stay on and become a member of that village, no one can prevent it. If he declares his desire to stay on in the new village, he is formally made a member of the village. And by the law of the land, no one, even at a later stage, can raise a finger to say that he or his children or the generations that follow do not belong to the village originally or that his family line joined the village much later. That silence should be maintained. If anyone breaks that silence, a heavy penalty is levied on that person.'

Grandmother stopped to catch her breath, while her

grandson looked at her, wondering about the Japanese soldiers. But before he could ask for clarification, she started again.

'There are also people who migrate to different villages. They may not have committed any offence, but for want of change they sometimes move. If they find a willing host village, they are free to be adopted into that village. Sometimes, family lines are also formed that way. Often smaller clans are open to accepting such families. Now, the previous law that I spoke of applies here, too. Do you understand what I'm saying?'

Her grandson nodded.

'The story of the Japanese soldiers is also the same. They have become part of us. They have ceased to be Japanese.'

There was a brief silence. The boy wondered if the law of silence should be maintained now and if he should refrain from asking further questions about the Japanese soldiers. But he was still curious to know more. 'Which are the villages that adopted them?' Even as he asked the question, he began to run through the families he knew in the village and he zeroed in on an old man whose language sounded funny. He had always wondered why his speech was very different from the rest of the people. People jocularly called him 'japanee', referring to the way he spoke, and he never minded. Could he really be a descendant of a Japanese soldier? Should he ask his grandmother such a direct question?

'Now that's where you've crossed the line!' joked

the old woman, at which both of them laughed. But she added, 'There is nothing wrong in knowing, but one should not utter it with the intention of maligning someone. Do you understand?'

'Yes.'

'I know you are asking if there are families in our village too.' Now she's got me, thought the boy. He smiled at her. But she also knew that her grandson meant Phyabu, the original village, as their village, Phyamaichi, was formed only after the villagers had converted to Christianity in 1944, the year the Japanese marched through their land.

'No. The Japanese soldiers did not manage to come this far. Most of the stories concern the Angami, Chakhesang and Mao areas.'

The story of the Japanese ended there. Grandmother said she was tired and retired to bed. Rakovei also went to lie down to sleep. But there was a new awakening in the mind of the young boy. A kind of time travel had begun. The theatre of WWII was recreated in his imagination. From the land of the rising sun the soldiers were marching onwards, some through the conquered land of China, some through the sea overtaking the nations of Southeast Asia. Soon they began to penetrate the jungles of Thailand and Burma. And then they were crossing the Naga country. But by then, the harsh weather in the rugged mountains had drained their strength away. They were merely stooping bodies walking to their death.

Chapter 10

Grandmother's wait for good news turned out to be a long and weary one. It was some days later that she saw her son Khole alight from one of the 'Imphal to Senapati' buses. She had been looking for the jeep that had taken the three of them to Imphal. Her son's face told her she should prepare for the worst. Her grandson had left for school, but he would be home soon.

'I was expecting all of you,' she said. 'What happened? What did the doctor say?'

'They said the head wound would heal soon. They didn't find it serious, as we thought,' began Khole. He knew it would be easier for his mother to take in the better news first. But the more distressing news followed right away. 'The doctors said Lenny's problem is related to the back pain about which he complained.'

'What is it, Khole?'

'It's an injury to the spinal cord. They said there is a dislocation of the spinal cord somewhere near the waist.'

'How serious is that?'

'It is serious. And they are not even sure if they can

help him at RIMS. If they can't treat Lenny there, we may have to take him somewhere far,' he said. He did not need to add that this would incur more expense. Though they were not considered poor, neither were they rich. Khole was the first in the family to be a government employee. And most families in the village were like them. Though they owned paddy fields and *khu*, a patch of forest, they could hardly consider them as wealth in terms of financial value. Nevertheless, Khole could only think of depending on them now.

'I think we should spread the word in the village if anyone is interested in any of our paddy fields or a part of our *khu*,' said Khole. 'I can't think of any other means. Which one would you like to offer first?'

There didn't seem to be any other option to get the money. The way Khole put things, he seemed to have mulled over it on his long journey on the bus. His mother sat silent, still stunned at the news of her second son's prospects. Both of them knew the only option was to sell a field or a part of the *khu*. Borrowing money privately was another option. But the steep interest rates and the uncertainty of being able to pay it back kept them from considering that option.

Meanwhile, Rakovei had returned from school. Finding that only his father had come back, he was also distressed. But he didn't want to barge into the talk that the mother and son were having. So he quietly slipped into the kitchen and helped himself to some food.

'Whom can we offer?' Grandmother said after some

time. She was more concerned about finding takers. 'How much would they give for half of the field at *duphao*? Or for the *khu* at *laonya*?' Her attachment to those traditionally passed-down patches of land or forest was certainly as close as her children. They deliberated on the topic and identified a few people they could approach. Accordingly, word was sent to the village.

The next day, early in the morning, Khole headed back to Imphal.

That day, schools in and around Senapati town planned to hold a protest march against the atrocities committed by the Assam Rifles in the areas affected by Operation Bluebird, and against the crippled civil administration because of the army's excessive use of power in the entire district. Some of Rakovei's teachers at Don Bosco School who were from some of the affected villages had proposed the idea. Word was passed on to other schools. Earlier that year, Bethany High School had been established and it became the first private school in and around Senapati town. Its boarding facility had attracted lots of students from the villages, many of whom were from the affected areas. And when the call for protest came, they were emotionally drawn to the cause and offered to make the placards to be used on the day of the protest. Then there was the Government High School, but it had only a few students, like many of the dying government schools elsewhere.

The students from the three schools soon gathered at the playground, which was just above the highway overlooking the town. Rakovei and his friend, wearing their school uniform—a pair of blue pants, a white shirt and a blue tie—were giggling at the prospect of missing classes for a few hours. But his spirit dampened when he saw the soldiers who glared at the students as though they were nothing but troublemakers. The football ground was filled with makeshift tents to house the extra soldiers, too numerous to find space in the regular camps, and also their vehicles. Ever since the assault on his uncle, Rakovei had nursed an anger that seemed to grow every time he encountered the men in uniform. His dream of becoming an army officer had faded away.

All the students had come in their own uniforms and were to march down the entire stretch of the highway and come back to the ground for the final shouting of slogans. Being informed of the protest, the local police had stopped the traffic flow in the town for an hour. At ten o'clock, the silent protest started. They walked down the middle of the highway, with placards held up between three or four students. The placards read: 'Down with Military Rule', 'Stop Looting the Granaries', 'Stop Killing Innocent People', 'Down with the Assam Rifles', 'Army Rule, No Thanks', 'We Want Justice', 'Shame, Shame, Operation Bluebird', 'Stop Torturing Innocent Villagers' and 'Army Rule = Human Rights Violations'. With the sun burning down on them, some students used the placards as shields against the heat. For once, without vehicles plying along the NH 39, the town seemed to have joined the students in the silent protest. Shopkeepers stood outside their shops and joined the shoppers who had suddenly become onlookers. From a safe distance, many stared hard to read the writing on the placards and often nodded in agreement. A couple of people took pictures of the protest. Some of them seemed to have come representing the press. An hour later, the students went back to the playground. One young teacher led the shouting of slogans and the students joined in. A couple of teachers were standing on the sides and encouraged the students to raise their pitch. But the release of the traffic suddenly engulfed the shouts of the children screaming their lungs out. Though the highway did not normally have much traffic, an hour of blockage just outside the town had piled up vehicles, which now flowed into the town as though they were joined together.

Half an hour later, the protest ended. The exasperated children rushed to the corner where drinking water had been made ready for them. After a while they dispersed, heading to their own schools. A couple of the teachers were seen talking to the reporters. Just as they were heading towards their school, Rakovei paused for a few seconds to listen to a familiar sound. As he turned towards the highway, his eyes met the familiar sight of the military convoy riding up the NH 39. It was just the ordinary fleet of vehicles, except that they were headed up north along the highway, unlike the ones that usually came down. He stood still to listen to the rhythmic sound, but for once he couldn't feel the vibration because he was not at home. He was a bit too far away to feel it.

The next day, the English dailies carried some photos and reports of the previous day's protest. Taking their cue from the students, public organizations too decided to hold a protest the following week to show their unity against the excessive actions of the Assam Rifles. The Senapati unit of the NPMHR spearheaded the mobilization of people to join the protest. It turned out to be a big success, with more press attention paid to them. And more protests followed.

Sanei took the evening bus and came home. One of them was required to stay at the hospital all the time, so husband and wife took turns to come. But her coming home this time had a reason other than the mere need to report, which could have been done over the phone.

'The doctors said that some treatment can be administered at the hospital for now. That is good news.'

That brought relief for the grandmother and grandson who were keenly listening to her. But the relief was short lived as she continued, 'However, they said it may be a slow recovery. They warned us not to bring him back here even though he could be discharged in a few days' time. They said his movement should be restricted and he will need to go to the hospital frequently for the first few months so the doctors can check on his progress.'

'What do we do then?' inquired the worried grandmother. But her daughter-in-law had some good news ready.

'Do you remember my cousin Sheye, Uncle Daphya's daughter, from the bigger village? They stay at Poumai colony, Chingmeirong. She and her husband paid a visit yesterday after they learned of Lenny. And when they heard from the doctor about his condition, they offered a room at their house. In fact, they insisted on it.'

'Really? That was very generous of them! But wouldn't it be too much trouble for them?'

'It will be. But Khole and I think it is a better option than staying in a hotel. Anyway, we don't know how long we will be required to stay in Imphal,' Sanei said. 'Khole wants both of you to come with me tomorrow so that you can meet Sheye and her family when we move Lenny to their place.'

So the next day, the three of them caught the early morning bus to Imphal. By midday Lenny was ready to be discharged from hospital. He seemed to have recovered to a good extent and everyone was happy about it. But the MRI report had revealed that the lower vertebrae of his spinal cord were badly injured. The doctors had told Khole earlier that day that a complete recovery would be difficult. They also warned that there was a high chance that parts of his lower body could be numb, which would eventually lead to partial paralysis. His was a case of severe spinal cord injury, the doctors said.

They hired a taxi and moved him to Sheye's place at Poumai colony. Grandmother was surprised to find many people there whom she knew. When she saw the many well-wishers, some of whom were Lenny's friends, who had come to visit her son, she was touched and felt very emotional. That day she and Khole stayed over, but Sanei had to go back with her son because of his school.

Days and weeks went by, but as expected Lenny's recovery was slow. However, the number of visits to the hospital decreased and Lenny was able to rest. Sitting in a wheelchair, he could move slowly. And a few months later, he was brought to Senapati on the doctor's advice, as visits to the hospital would now only be when needed. By then the family had sold a paddy field and a *khu*. Grandmother had aged considerably in that time. That year, both Grandmother and Lenny celebrated Christmas in town. Despite the trouble that had come upon them, Rakovei was quite happy that his uncle and grandmother could enjoy Christmas with them. By March of the next year, Lenny was ready to be moved back to the village. 'There are more hands in the village,' Grandmother would say, insisting on going to the village. Besides, she was worried that she would be too late for the seed-planting season. Even though she had stopped doing major agricultural work, she still loved to engage herself in the garden. She would complain that she felt sickly without some physical activity.

Chapter 11

One afternoon some months later, Grandmother quietly showed up at the doorstep of her son at Senapati. Only Sanei was at home. Khole had gone to office and Rakovei hadn't returned from school. This was towards the close of 1989. Surprised, her daughter-in-law exclaimed, 'Oh! You didn't send word of your coming! Is everything all right in the village?'

'I know. But no one was travelling in the last few days through whom I could send word to you.'

With no telephone in the village, there was no way to pass on messages if people were not travelling. Though most households in the village had completed the harvest, they were still busy storing the crop. Since she wasn't tilling fields she was free to travel. The lone paddy field, her younger son's rightful inheritance, was given to a family in the village and in return some tins of paddy would be given as their share. Lenny's health had improved even though he was still bound to the wheelchair. Shiveine had volunteered to look after her brother while their mother was gone for a few days.

'Don't tell me you travelled alone to Paomata Centre!'

'No, no. I wouldn't do that. Someone was going till Paomata for some work, so I joined him.'

'How's Lenny doing?'

'He's improved a lot. He can do a few small tasks wherever he can reach. But since he's immobile from the waist down on the left side, he's perpetually tied to the wheelchair.' Grandmother hesitated, then added, 'But it's not about him that I've come.'

'I can sense that,' said Sanei. She went to the other room where the telephone was kept. 'Just a minute. Let me tell Khole that you have come.'

Sanei then busied herself making a stew of dried herbs in the kitchen while her mother-in-law rested in the bedroom. Khole came fifteen minutes after the phone call.

'*Hei*, you needn't have left office! It wasn't that urgent!' his mother said, seeing her son.

'That's all right. There wasn't much to do at office today,' he said.

Over the afternoon meal, Grandmother began the conversation. 'You may not have heard, but Rakhune hasn't been quite herself in the last few months. Everyone is worried about her.' Rakhune was Khole's first cousin. She and her family used to stay in Dimapur, but came to live in the village after her husband died. The story of how Daniel, her husband, died was very sad as he was killed by one of his own. At the beginning of 1988, differences cropped up within the NSCN, leading to a bloody split within the nationalist organization.

The news came as a shock to everyone everywhere. The NSCN was only formed in 1980 and had barely gained strength. But within a span of eight years, it was battling itself. People overground never knew why and how it happened. All they knew was of the deaths of their loved ones who had gone to join the 'freedom struggle', now brought home one by one, killed by their own people. All they knew was that there was misunderstanding among the three top leaders which had flared up into a factional war.

When the NSCN was formed in 1980, Isak Chishi Swu, a Sema Naga, S.S. Khaplang, a Hemi Naga (from Burma), and Th Muivah, a Tangkhul Naga, respectively became President, Vice-President and Secretary of the organization. But in 1988 differences arose among them, for reasons best known to them, and a bloody fight was fought in the jungles of Burma, resulting in the killing of hundreds of their cadres. The result was the split of the NSCN into NSCN-IM led by Isak Chishi Swu and Th Muivah, and NSCN-K led by S.S. Khaplang. Cadres spread far and wide were compelled to choose which leaders to follow.

It was during this time of uncertainty that Daniel was killed along with his younger brother Khapulou, who had come to visit him at his Dimapur home. The plains of Dimapur had become popular for the UGs and businessmen alike to make a fresh beginning. In principle, the families of the UGs were encouraged to settle down there. So when Daniel got married a few years ago, he brought his wife to his modest house in the warmer plains. Being close to Lenny, Daniel would spend time with him whenever he went to the village. During those times, he would coax his friend to join the newly formed NSCN, much to the worry of Lenny's family members. But after he got married, Daniel was engaged between his own UG activities and his new family at Dimapur. But as rumours of problems broiling in their HQ in the forests of Burma grew, people like him were pressured to choose between the polarized leaders. Soon it escalated into an ugly factional war. Each group was targeting the other by trying their best to eliminate the Judases. When Daniel showed signs of inclination to go towards the K group, his colleagues, who all leaned towards the IM, tried to persuade him to be on the stronger side. His long association with the nationalist movement since the NNC days had placed him in a higher position, though he had barely managed to pass Class V. At the time when trouble erupted, he was commanding a regional army of the NSCN. Though he knew IM was the stronger group, he was offered a better position in the K. People close to him suspected that he had something brewing. But since he had not openly spoken of it, no action could be taken.

When his younger brother came visiting one day, Daniel took the opportunity to involve him in his plans. Hurriedly they hid Daniel's team's weapons. The next day he planned to report to the nearest K camp.

Unfortunately, his plan was never put into action, nor were the hidden weapons recovered. That evening some IM men raided his house and took them by surprise. They barged in through the front door. His younger brother brought down one of them bare-handed while shouting, 'Run, Daniel, run!' Daniel tried to escape through the window, but was felled by bullets shot by the other men guarding the house from outside. The adversary had come well prepared and executed the attack precisely. In a few minutes the job was done. And like they came, they vanished into the dusk. Rakhune, who was nursing her eight-month-old daughter, dropped the baby on the bed and came rushing out of the bedroom. Her two-year-old son was rudely woken from his nap by the sound of gunshots. She shrieked at the sight of the bloodied body of her brother-in-law on the kitchen floor. Not finding her husband, she called, 'Daniel', and took another step towards the wide-open window. Then her heart skipped a beat at the sight of her husband's lifeless body outside in the kitchen garden. She collapsed. When she regained consciousness, a few of her neighbours had gathered inside their house.

'The thing is,' Grandmother said, 'with both Daniel and his brother dead and their three sisters married with children, there is no one to look after Daniel and Rakhune's children. The children's grandparents are already too old to take care of the young ones. And from Rakhune's side too, none of the siblings is willing to take on the extra responsibility of raising someone's kids when their hands are full. That is why I've come to ask if you would be willing to adopt Rakhune's children now that her mental instability seems to have become more frequent. She cannot look after them—that much is certain.'

Both husband and wife were shocked to hear of Rakhune's condition. For some seconds, they sat silently trying to digest what Grandmother had said. Khole knew that it was his moral duty to shoulder the responsibility if the immediate family refused to come to his cousin's help. After a while he spoke with heavy heart, 'Is she that badly affected? Oh God, why has all this happened to her! Is she with her parents or at her in-laws?'

'She's with her parents now, with the children. Initially, she was staying with her in-laws but the trauma was too much for all of them,' said Grandmother.

'Have you had some words with others too on this matter?'

'Both sides have no problem. In fact, it was Hreile, her brother, who brought the matter to me, but it was Lenny, you know how close he was to Rakhune, who insisted that I come here and discuss it with your family.'

'Have you tried talking about this when she's normal?'

'Of course. As a mother she's very emotional about it. Who would want to part from one's own children? I have a strong feeling that an assurance from you would be good. The older child ought to be in school by now.'

'Personally, I will be happy to keep the children,' interjected Sanei. 'But I think it is a good idea to talk it over as a family after Rakovei returns home.' She knew that her husband would also love to have them. After all, they had always wanted more kids. It wasn't their choice to have only one child, it only turned out that way. In the first two years of their marriage, they had been really worried about having a child, but thankfully their son was conceived as they entered the third year of their marriage. Now their only son was a teenager and wanted to be consulted about family matters. When he came home after school, he too was surprised to find his grandmother, and very pleased with what awaited him at the dinner table. There was a bowl full of small field grasshoppers that his grandmother had brought from the village. She had dry cooked them, and they looked delicious.

'Did you catch them yourself?' he teased his grandmother.

'No! Do I have the energy to run after them? It was your cousins, Chizüne and Rakho, who caught them. That's the outcome of their labour during one afternoon.'

'That's nice of them. Please thank them for me. How I wish I could join them. I never get the chance to go home at this time of year.' There were no holidays in October and November, and nor was there any prospect of free time before Christmas. This is when

I miss people in the village, he thought. The post-harvest period was a time of much fun for the village kids. Besides the last few seasonal fruits still hanging on the trees, catching the small grasshoppers in the now harvested paddy fields was a game to relish. The children ran in groups after the grasshoppers in a catch-me-if-you-can game. They ignored the cuts all over their shins and thighs from the long stalks of the paddy. Of course, they would scream with pain when their parents forced them to take a bath in the evening and to apply glycerin.

That evening after dinner, Sanei started by teasingly asking her son if he would like to have more siblings. Rakovei was a bit embarrassed because he thought his mother was about to announce her pregnancy. So he asked her why she had posed such a question. When his mother explained the situation, he experienced mixed emotions. He was excited because as a kid he had always wanted siblings and still remembered asking his mother to give him one so that he could be like his friends who all had siblings. But he wasn't sure if he wanted small kids in the house now—they would mess up all his things. Yet he was also sympathetic to the plight of his aunt Rakhune.

The next day, his father proposed that they all go to the village for Christmas that year, and also meet the two children and their mother. After Lenny's injury, the family had decided to be by his side whenever they could, especially during times of celebration.

That winter, the family's vacation in Phyamaichi

was driven by a mission. The day after their arrival the family visited Rakhune and her two kids in their house which was located in the middle of the village. But just as they were stepping into Rakhune's compound, they heard an ominous sound and stopped short. It was the sound of Rakhune mourning in the backyard, a low wailing sound, as though she had been drained of all her strength. They all stood motionless, not knowing whether they should proceed into the house or go back. After a few minutes, they decided to come back later and retraced their steps.

Later that day, they met Rakhune's parents who told them that of late her behaviour had become erratic. Now they could not predict when she might become unstable. Sometimes she turned violent and looked for *daos* and knives, saying she would kill the culprits hiding in the backyard. At times she shrieked and rushed to protect her children, fearing that the killers had come to kill them too. Her behaviour made the children cry out in fear. No one knew how to deal with her. All that people could do was sympathize with the family and feel sorry for Rakhune.

After some days, however, Rakhune returned to normal and welcomed them, talking cheerfully as though everything was all right and as though she had overcome the trauma. But she had changed immensely. She appeared drained of all her inner strength, as though she carried an invisible load. There were times when she wouldn't eat or sleep for days and nights, her parents said. Everyone around her had been dragged into her painful world.

Rakovei soon became acquainted with the two kids, Chasü, who was three and a half years old, and Veine, who was two years old. The younger child had an innocent smile, but the older child tended to be moody. Perhaps the memory of his father's gruesome murder still lingered, even though he had been just two years old at the time. His mother's mentally disturbed state made his condition worse. When Rakhune's depression deepened, her children were taken to a cousin's home. Her often violent hallucinations made everyone worry about the children.

One day, Khole and Sanei went to meet Rakhune to discuss the future of her children. Putting aside their apprehensions, they entered the house. Rakhune was cleaning some vegetables for the evening meal. Over the three standing stones in the fireplace was a kettle of boiling water. Sunshine poured in through a small window, providing the only source of light in the house. After Rakhune served them tea and they had a general conversation, Khole broached the topic they had come to discuss. 'Rakhune, I know you must have thought this over. What are your plans about sending the children to school?'

Rakhune immediately understood the purpose of their visit. She burst into tears. 'I know what you mean... my parents tried to talk to me about it. But please...I can't, I can't think of it...' She cried like a small baby whose toy was being taken away. Sanei went to her and gave her a shoulder to lean on, and she cried till she was exhausted. Husband and wife didn't have words to console her, and listened to her cry as if the tears were her words. They couldn't say anything more and left after a while, despite her seemingly having regained her composure. How could they watch her tears?

But the next morning, the family was surprised by a visit from Rakhune. She seemed embarrassed by her behaviour the previous day. 'I'm sorry about yesterday,' she said softly.

'You don't have to say that, dear,' said Sanei with a smile, leading her to a wooden seat. As on any winter morning, they were all gathered around the fireplace in the middle of the kitchen.

'I know you all mean to do the best for my children,' Rakhune said with controlled emotion. 'My poor son already has suffered too much from seeing his *puo* die so wretchedly. And now having to see me become this...' Suddenly she couldn't resist the tears. 'It would be best for him not to see me like this.' She now seemed to have resigned herself to the overpowering force of her delusions. But before she got lost she added, 'Initially, when my parents and siblings discussed this matter, I got very furious and accused them of trying to take my precious little ones from me. But when I regained my sanity, I thought over it. I want my children to grow up in a secure and loving home and to have a future.'

'You shouldn't think that we are trying to take your children from you forever. They will always be your children, Rakhune,' said Khole.

'Don't call me Rakhune, the one with whom God is pleased, anymore,' she sharply cut in. 'Call me Rachapfüe, the one who has been cursed by God. There's nothing left of me. I'm cursed.'

'You are not cursed. All that happened was the result of men's action, not God's,' he reprimanded her. But his wife nudged him with her elbow, warning him not to get preachy at a time like this.

Thankfully, Lenny jumped in to the rescue. He and Rakhune had always been the closest of the cousins, and her marriage to his best friend was partly his doing. Since Daniel was in the UG, there had been little time for him to woo her, but he had always liked her since they were in school together. And the few times he came home, he would always prevail upon her cousin to arrange some dates. He would send love letters, to which she began responding, and soon they fell in love.

'Look at me, Rakhu,' Lenny said. 'I've been maimed for life. Had I been normal, I would personally take responsibility for the wellbeing of the three of you. But that is not possible. I told *apfü* to personally take the initiative to talk to the others and told her to go to the town and speak to my elder brother's family. It will be good, especially for my nephew Chasü to have the company of a big brother so that he will forget the memory of his father's death.'

Lenny's words were soothing to Rakhune. Accordingly, two days later, Chasü was allowed to move to Senapati for school, but Veine would stay for some time with her mother as she was still too young to go to school.

CHAPTER 12

Time went by swiftly. With the start of the new school session in February, Chasü was admitted to KG-I at Don Bosco School. It became Rakovei's responsibility to drop his new brother in the morning, even though the higher classes from Class III onwards were held in a different campus, a bit further up, towards Katomai village. Mother had to pick up Chasü since the lower classes finished early. Besides, being in Class IX, Rakovei was expected to put in more efforts because the final exam would also be the basis of selection to Class X, and so on alternate days he would stay back for extra coaching classes with some of his friends.

The year 1990 was memorable for a couple of reasons for the boy. The best of it was the FIFA World Cup. He had heard of Diego Maradona's fame in the football world, but hadn't had an opportunity to see his hero in action on TV so far. His father too was a football fan, so just before the commencement of the World Cup, he bought a standard size Onida black and white television. TV was a luxury then, and many friends and neighbours visited their house to see some of the matches when the countries they supported were scheduled to play. Maradona had many fans even in this remote part of the world. The short but well-built footballer mesmerized his admirers with his skills, dribbling the ball past the tall opposition defenders. However, the heavyweight football nations like Italy, Brazil, England and West Germany had many diehard fans. Many of them wouldn't have known where all those countries were located on the world map, but that didn't matter, they were great footballing nations. Often, his father would allow people to watch TV even during the day, when the highlights of the match of the previous night were repeated. Sometimes Mother would complain about the crowds. But Father would pacify her, 'The World Cup is played only once in four years, let them be.' Not everyone could afford a TV set and so they enjoyed being able to watch the beautiful game. Some would even stand the whole time, transfixed by the little box, screaming with joy whenever their team scored a goal. Unfortunately, their favourite, Argentina, despite its star Maradona, lost to West Germany one-zero in the final. Everyone wept with Maradona at the end.

That year, the town attracted many more students from different villages in the district, particularly after the establishment of another private school called Mt. Everest School by a couple, V. Alexander Pao and V. Esther, who were both from Phyamaichi. Though it was an initiative of an individual family, the entire village looked upon it as some kind of community enterprise, and many families happily sent their children to the hostel run by the school. The proprietors of the school, who had taught before at schools in Imphal, were able to give a good start to their school and it soon became well known. Even students from neighbouring districts like Tamenglong and Ukhrul soon sought admission. The new private schools in town began to attract many more students than expected, as if people were just waiting for schools to sprout so that they could send their children to study. The next few years saw the founding of even more private schools. And yet there was no dearth of students. The emergence and popularity of these private schools reflected the sorry state of the government-run schools.

The deteriorating condition of government schools affected the poor families in the villages in particular. While the well-to-do families could afford to send their kids to the upcoming private schools in the towns, many poor families were forced to withdraw their children from school and have them take up work in the paddy fields and farms. Reports about the poor conditions in schools in the interior of the state compelled the state government to take some action and to upgrade and downgrade the schools accordingly. In the case of the Government High School at Phyamaichi, which until recently had been a full-fledged high school (up to Class X), it was downgraded to a junior high school (up to Class VIII). Many of the problems resulted from the rapidly dwindling number of teachers, many of whom had little experience, especially those who were not native to the village. The government hardly did anything to check the problem of teacher absenteeism. The people helplessly watched the slow death of the government schools. Following the shortage of teachers in the initial stages, the schools now began to run short of students.

However, Rakovei was happy that many of his acquaintances from the village had come to town to pursue their studies. He didn't understand the plight of those in the village who had been forced to relocate to the town for want of good schools. Many of them became boarders at Mt. Everest School, while some with older siblings rented houses in the town. Rakovei was pleased as his circle of friends grew. Chizüne, now that she had to be admitted to Class IX, got the chance to experience town life. But since Mt. Everest School in the initial years was only till Class VIII, she and a few of her batch mates were admitted to Bethany High School.

Rakho implored his parents to allow him to join his sister in town, but his parents insisted that he stay for another year to complete Class VIII at the village school. When the much-awaited next year finally arrived, he was very excited to be heading to town. His parents wanted him to join Mt. Everest. Perhaps they felt a bond with the proprietors for being from the same village. So Chizüne was pulled out of the school hostel and the two siblings found a small place behind their cousin's house. That way Rakovei's parents could keep an eye on them too.

That year, the little girl, Veine, joined her brother in their new family. There was no sign of improvement in Rakhune's mental health.

A year later, there was a celebration in the house. Rakovei had matriculated! But the happiness also came with a catch. The boy would soon leave home since no school in Senapati town had classes beyond the tenth standard. When asked where he would like to go, he was in a fix. Finally, he decided to follow the majority of his classmates and go to Imphal. Though he sometimes contemplated joining some of his friends who had gone to Shillong and Guwahati, he decided he didn't want to be too far from Senapati since this would be his first time away from home. When the new academic session began in July, he enrolled at MBC Higher Secondary School. He found a boys' hostel close by. Soon he began to experience a new life. He missed home terribly during the first few weeks and silently cried at night, trying to hide from his friends for fear that they would laugh at him. A couple of times, Father dropped by to check on his son, but Rakovei felt a little shy expressing his real feelings. However, he slowly got used to it and began to find life away from home exciting.

One day at the beginning of the first week of December, he called home excitedly. '*Pfü*, school will be closed in a week's time. I'm dying to come home.'

'That's wonderful!' Mother answered, happy that her son would be home after a long absence. She had wanted to visit him, but she couldn't manage to get away because of the other two kids at home. 'Should I tell your *puo* to come and get you? What date would be good?' she asked.

'That's all right. I will come home with some friends. We can travel together,' he said, surprising his mother. She had forgotten that her son was growing up fast. Later she informed her husband about their son's plans.

Two days later, however, an incident occurred in Moreh that spread panic across the state. What began as a business rivalry between some Kuki and Naga individuals soon grew into full-blown ethnic violence between the two groups. Within days, they were counting the deaths. Each group blamed the other for the violence. The failure to contain the violence within the town where it all started meant that the quarrel soon escalated into a full-scale ethnic clash between the Kukis and the Nagas. Most people did not know how it all began exactly, but nobody seemed to be bothered about this. Both the groups had spread their own version of the story.

A few days before the school closed for the winter vacation, Rakovei was shocked to read the news in the newspaper. According to the account, a few Kukis travelling on the tourist buses to Imphal were forcibly pulled out by the Nagas on the NH 39 and were suspected to have been killed. This, the newspaper reported, was retaliation for similar acts committed elsewhere by the Kukis. Following this, the Kuki organizations called for an indefinite *bandh* along the highway. Rakovei's plans of going home suddenly became uncertain. What made things worse was the fact that the UGs from both the communities had begun to get directly involved in the matter.

One thing led to another in quick succession. Longtime neighbours abruptly found themselves caught in awkward situations. Like bad air that affects everyone in the environment, the violence affected even friends. In Rakovei's class, Naga and Kuki friends avoided each other. Though it was no fault of their own, they were nevertheless made to feel guilty. Teachers sensed the growing estrangement, but were not sure how to deal with it. Being a Christian school, the principal tried to spread the message about the importance of oneness, but it had no effect. Just when Rakovei had almost lost hope of being able to go home, there was welcome news that the two ethnic groups had called for a truce during the week of Christmas and New Year, a temporary victory achieved by the Christian mission workers who had sought to defuse the tension. It was funny, though, that even a serious situation involving deaths could be put on hold, like children's play. For many who were stuck far from home, it was an opportune moment to go home.

On Christmas Eve, Rakovei boarded the bus to Senapati along with some friends after calling home and telling his parents of his travel plans. Despite the declaration of ceasefire, there was widespread suspicion and tension. They all prayed hard that they would reach home safely. Both the Kukis and the Nagas live interlaced along the highway, so no one from the two communities could consider themselves safe. As the bus went past the hostel in which he stayed, he sighed with relief. But at Sekmai, the last town dominated by Meiteis and the last leg before the highway crawled up the hills, the bus abruptly stopped. The driver murmured something and climbed down from his seat. Since the youngsters were seated towards the back of the bus, they didn't hear what was said between the bus driver and his interlocutors on the ground. They thought the driver had got down to buy something, but when it took longer than expected, one of them asked someone sitting on the front seat what was going on. The person replied that the bus was waiting for the military convoy. Then they understood the reason for the long delay. When Rakovei peeked out through the rear window, he saw a couple of other buses also lined up. Half an hour later, the military convoy appeared. The driver hopped into his seat and called out, 'Is everyone in?' Hearing no response, the conductor blew his whistle and the bus slowly inched its way into a gap between two military vehicles.

Soon they drove past some Kuki villages. Strangely, they did not look too tense or threatening. It was so different from what Rakovei had thought. Or was the apparent peace because of the military convoy? For the first time in many years, he felt the presence of the Assam Rifles comforting. Ever since the ugly encounter with them five years ago, he had grown more and more cynical about the presence of the uniformed men everywhere. For a long time, his childhood dream of becoming an army officer had blinded him to the reality. Now, every time he encountered them, whether their bus was stopped on the highway for a thorough check while on the way to the village or while occasionally accompanying his parents to Dimapur or Imphal, he saw it as unnecessary harassment. Was it his coming of age that had made him see the situation in a new light? Did everybody see it that way? He remembered asking his parents once during one of the random checks on the highway by the Assam Rifles, 'Why do they always check us like this all the time?' His father wasn't surprised that his son had grown to ask such questions. 'Son, what can I say? They think they are doing their duty looking for UGs, as if the UGs will be hiding on public transport with their guns. What is even worse is that these soldiers are much too powerful to be answered back by common people like us. We just have to let them have their way. And if this bus doesn't stop for them, it will be severely penalized the next time it passes through.' There was angst in the answer his father gave, but he couldn't read his mind. The young boy wanted to ask for an explanation about certain things that his father had hinted at, but he remained silent.

Perhaps one day he would get to know the actual facts. But the questions still hovered in his mind.

While he was still lost in thought, the bus had travelled a long distance. He realized they were already in Kangpokpi, the last town dominated by the Kukis before the final destination. As the bus slowed down, he felt people were staring at him maliciously. Or was his mind playing games? He couldn't be sure. To relieve the tension, he turned away from the window. He saw his friend in the next seat was fast asleep. How could he rest peacefully at such a time? He almost shook him awake, but then stopped himself. After the bus crossed Kangpokpi, he felt much lighter, as though a heavy weight had been lifted from his shoulders. Soon he felt he was racing with the bus to reach home in a hurry.

When the bus finally entered Senapati town, Rakovei glanced through the window and found his parents standing on the porch of their home, looking anxiously at the buses arriving from Imphal. That they had been waiting for quite some time was reflected in their faces. When they saw him, they smiled with relief. 'What took the bus so long?' asked his mother.

'Was it that long? I thought it reached earlier than the usual time. We had to stop at Sekmai for half an hour and wait for the army convoy to pass. After that, it really didn't stop on the way because we were following the convoy.'

'Really? We were hoping you would arrive an hour earlier.'

But having realized that the wait might have seemed longer because of tension, she focused on the fact that her son was home safe and sound. His father asked him a different question, 'Whom did you come with?'

'Three of my friends, two of them from the same hostel.'

'Are they also from the town? Why don't you invite them in for a cup of tea? Just in case they're not from here and have to travel further?'

Rakovei had not really thought about this. He had been too busy thinking of getting home. 'I think two of them are from here, but I don't know about the other. I should have asked, no?' He felt a little stupid. What must they be thinking of me, he thought, that I was so anxious to get home that I forgot all about them? Anyway, it was too late now. He would make amends the next time.

At home, his two siblings were happy to see him. 'You both seem to have grown so big in just half a year of my absence!' he cried. They giggled at the praise from their big brother. That evening the family had a Christmas Eve celebration over a big local-bred chicken. He thoroughly enjoyed home food after such a long time. He hadn't realized how much he missed home!

Meanwhile, the Naga-Kuki conflict went from bad to worse. Though there was a little respite during Christmas time, the dawn of the new year brought more bad news for both the communities. As the months progressed, the death toll reported rose by hundreds.

Villages were uprooted and people were displaced. Though most people in these villages had lived side by side for decades, the sudden turn of events had turned them into foes overnight. From a small incident that could have been quelled had the government paid more attention, the conflict soon took the form of broader identity politics. Since the Nagas and Kukis were both hill communities, the effect was felt more in the hill districts of the state, especially Ukhrul, Tamenglong, Senapati and Chandel. For some time the government, seated in the valley district of Imphal, could not entirely grasp the intensity of the conflict. Perhaps the hills were too far for it to notice, though villages were being burned down. Or perhaps it thought it was just the smoke from the burning of *jhum* cultivation. Or was it callousness arising out of the growing divide between the hills and the valley? Whatever it was, the government woke up only when the wound was deep. The healing of it was not going to be easy.

Though Rakovei was able to travel back to his hostel in Imphal when school reopened, his parents remained concerned. He would often tell them, 'Don't worry, everything is as normal as it always has been here.' But when they read or heard of violence and killings in different districts in the newspaper or through the grapevine, they could not help but feel some uneasiness. Or perhaps the stories that Rakho brought from his school added to the worry. Mt. Everest School was just half a kilometre away from Kuki Taphou village, which had notoriously held its ground despite being vulnerable to the attacks by Nagas, as it was circled by Naga villages. Some said that the boldness of the villagers was because of the protection of the 9 Manipur Rifles camp just adjacent to it, where many Kukis held officers' posts. Some said the village had many of their UGs positioned for a counterattack in case of an emergency. Whatever the story, the situation was keeping the school uncomfortable, especially since many students lived in the hostel. Besides, when the new academic session started, no student from Kuki Taphou sought admission, thereby adding to the anxiety of the villagers who were worried that the village was planning to assault the school if the situation were to worsen. Earlier, the people of the village had lauded the establishment of the school since it would provide their children with a good education. But then the conflict had forced parents to pull their children out of the school for fear of repercussions despite assurances from the school authorities.

By the middle of 1992, the state security forces were on high alert, as tension continued to remain high. The families of most victims were determined to avenge the deaths of their loved ones and the villagers whose houses had been burned down were filled with bitterness. When Rakovei came home after his Class XI examination, he saw a huge change in the demography of the town in which he had grown up. Many unknown people now roamed about the town as though they had always been there. Many houses had come up on the river belt and houses had even sprouted across the river, which later formed a village called Ekailungdi. Senapati town became a haven for the Nagas who fled their homes and villages because of the conflict. The Naga public organizations made arrangements to help these fellow Nagas. Thangals and Liangmais made up the bulk of these populations, though substantial numbers were also from various other Naga tribes. The homes of many of these people had not been burned down, but they had run away out of fear, and sadly they could never go back to their original homes.

A few days after Rakovei came home that summer, the family woke up to hear loud mourning that seemed to come from a neighbour's house. His father went out to investigate. Some minutes later, he returned with news that shocked everyone. 'Kaisa's husband has died,' he said.

'Oh, no! We didn't hear of him being sick,' Sanei said. She and Kaisa, a Mao woman who was married to a Kom, were partners in a small business besides being neighbours. The couple had three children; the youngest was good friends with Veine and was also her school partner.

'It seems Kaisa's husband was pulled down from a bus by some Naga youngsters on the highway. They killed him thinking he was a Kuki,' said Khole.

'What?' cried Rakovei and his mother in disbelief.

'How could that be? How do they know that our

people killed him? They should know that Koms are not Kukis!' Rakovei said. He spoke out of hurt because he also had some Kom friends in Imphal who professed to be Nagas. But he also knew that the Kom and some small communities living at the base of the hill districts and in the foothills of the valley were caught in the crossfire because their villages were inter-mingled with those of the warring tribes. Maintaining a neutral stand was becoming increasingly difficult. They were at the receiving end, fearing assault from both the parties at war.

'It was most certainly our people who did this because his body was found by the patrolling state police near a Naga village yesterday. Some months ago, the NSCN had asked different villages from all the tribes to send volunteers there with arms. Maybe his name had been misunderstood. The police identified him and delivered the body to his village as mentioned in his ID card. Early this morning, one of the relatives called to inform Kaisa.'

'This is terrible! I should go and see how things are,' Sanei said, rising from her seat. 'One of you take care of the cooking.'

After some time, Sanei returned, bringing the slain man's children with her so she could give them food. 'They were inconsolable, especially the older two,' she said. 'They understand what it means to be without a father.'

Similar stories of terrible events continued to haunt

the people for a long time. The conflict continued for another year or so. With much effort from churches and humanitarian organizations, the situation was brought under control and tempers were finally calmed down. But the hurt was deep and real, and the earlier relations shared by the two hill communities could not be restored. Though they all professed Christianity, its principle of reconciliation was overshadowed by human stubbornness and the inability or refusal to forgive and forget. Anyone preaching love and reconciliation ended up being scoffed at.

Chapter 13

When Rakovei heard that the results of his Class XII examinations were out, he experienced mixed feelings. While he was confident of passing, he did not expect very good results. He knew he hadn't done his best because of all the disturbances during the last two years. Calling a *bandh* had become the most popular method of public protest, not only against the government but also against anything that any organization was displeased with. And the student community was always at the receiving end. Every time a *bandh* was called, all educational institutions were shut down, either because vehicular movement was restricted or for fear of reprisals from those who had called for a *bandh*. Classes were canceled for days. But the schools would not arrange extra classes to make up for this, and the students suffered at the end. The calling of a *bandh* exposed the politics behind it. Sadly, Manipur became even more unstable at the beginning of the 1990s.

Although life in Imphal, with its frustrations as well as excitement at exploring a new life away from his parents, had been enjoyable, Rakovei was grateful that he had managed to cross another crucial level in his academic pursuits, even though the results may have been not that satisfactory. His only regret was that he missed a first division by only a few marks. If only I had worked a little harder, he thought. But there was nothing to be done now. In any case, he was glad that his higher secondary education had come to an end. He couldn't find another reason to stay on for college in the city.

His parents were of the same opinion. They left it to him to decide where he wanted to go for further studies. But that didn't quite help him, so he told them that he would like to go either to Shillong or Delhi. On consideration, his parents decided that Delhi would be better for him. Lately, many young people had been heading to the University of Delhi for further studies. Besides, the city attracted those who wanted to take the competitive examinations. So he got in touch with some friends who were also headed to Delhi and they all booked their tickets with the help of some seniors from school who had come home for the summer vacation.

But the family's happiness was marred by news that came from the village. They got a call from a clansman who had run down to Paomata Centre specifically to make a phone call to them, informing them that Rakhune had met with an unfortunate end. The family immediately hired a jeep to go to the village, much to the alarm of the two younger children who had been told that they were all going to the village so that Rakovei could say goodbye to their relatives there before leaving for Delhi. But as they neared the village, the adults told the truth to the two children lest they be too shocked when they arrived. Khole and Sanei tried their best to reassure the children, but it didn't help, and they began to cry. Even though they were very young and even though they had found a new home, memories of their mother lingered on. Chasü was especially inconsolable. Seeing his two younger siblings, Rakovei finally let go of his emotion too, which he had held in for so long.

On seeing the two children come home to say a final goodbye to their mother, people mourning her short life joined in a chorus for the sake of the two little ones. It broke the hearts of the beholders to see them. As she was laid in her coffin, Rakhune looked much younger. She was finally released from the increasingly harsh reality that she had to face with each passing day. Only after the burial did the older members of the family from Senapati come to know how she had died. They were told that she did not display signs of her usual mental disturbance in the last few days of her life. On the afternoon of the fateful day, she picked up her *rho*, the back-held basket with a head strap, telling her parents that she was going to *duphao* to check on the field water level and to collect some fodder for the young pig they were rearing from the stream alongside the fields. On her way back, she must have rested at the halfway mark, which was the usual resting place near a cliff. Her *rho* was found there, half-filled with the pig's fodder of wild leaves. Her body was found right below the cliff. Did she slip or did she jump? Nobody knew. When she failed to appear at the expected time, her parents spread the alarm. By the time her body was found at the foot of the cliff, her mouth and nose, oozing with blood, were infested with insects. Without a word, the mother of two left the world that could not offer her refuge. The family stayed on for another day before they returned to Senapati.

At the end of June, Rakovei went to Dimapur to catch the Brahmaputra Mail. This was his first train journey, so he was excited. He and his friends reached the lone platform early in the morning, arriving an hour early. Even the terrible smell arising from the rail tracks failed to dampen their excitement. The platform soon grew crowded. There were many youngsters like them, most of them likely headed towards the same destination. When the train finally arrived, they all climbed aboard their sleeper class coach with their luggage, not knowing what to expect. Within minutes, the coach was packed with people. Many had to stand because all the seats were taken. Despite the coolness of the morning, they perspired because of the humidity. The crowd inside the coach made things worse. But as the train's speed increased, the wind blowing in through the open windows brought some relief.

The beautiful plains of Assam were spread out before them. With fields stretching endlessly one after the other in roughly equal sizes, they looked like a chessboard on the ground. The monsoon rain had washed the dust off the trees and the leaves sparkled in the first rays of the morning sun. The train stopped for a long time at Guwahati, collecting more passengers while only a few de-boarded. Soon the train crossed the long straight bridge across the Brahmaputra River. As in every year around this time, the river had swollen to its peak. As the train passed the midway point, the river looked like a huge ocean, engulfing hillocks that looked like the heads of human beings drowning in the current. For a river whose breadth was wider than the length of the train, even its calmness was an awe-inspiring sight. And the huge masses of debris floating on it were a sure sign of its destructive force.

The youngsters looked in awed silence at the mighty Brahmaputra. Many of them were seeing the famous river for the first time. The last time Rakovei saw a river swollen beyond its normal magnitude was in 1989 when the Barak River flowing below Senapati town engulfed the surrounding low-lying areas and fields. That year it rained like the sky was angry at the earth, and had loosened its reservoirs to drown the earth. The little town came out and lined the highway to helplessly watch the river carry away low-lying houses, livestock, and even a few unfortunate human beings. The muddied waters were a sign of the ravages the river had caused along its path. That year, even the course of the river changed. But the Barak River was just a tiny stream compared to the mighty Brahmaputra. His grandmother used to tell a story about the river swelling and becoming disastrous, the old 'smear-headed snake' coming up to claim lives. According to the story, a lovely girl was given in marriage to a snake that transformed itself into a handsome man during the day. She met him one day in the forest while she was all alone gathering some wild jute for weaving. He appeared as a handsome man and insisted on helping her despite her protests. As she turned homeward, he promised to visit her that night. He kept his word and that night took her away. In due course of time the girl became pregnant and was allowed to visit her parents for the birth of the child. The girl's parents knew it was going to be an unusual birth. So, on the day she was due to give birth, a pot of boiling water was readied and she was asked to give birth into it. As expected, she birthed baby snakes, but they all fell into the pot of boiling water and died except for one that escaped, but with its head badly smeared. Since that time, people believed that the 'smear-headed snake' appeared whenever the river swelled to claim lives as revenge. Having grown up listening to such stories, Rakovei looked at the wide expanse of the Brahmaputra, wondering if the old 'smear-headed snake' would appear. But suddenly he became self-conscious about his curiosity and held himself back.

By the time the train entered the mainland of the country, the heat and humidity increased, as did the number of people. Soon various hawkers invaded the coaches to sell their cheap goods, many of which were branded to attract customers. With their smart talk and throwaway prices, the clever salesmen succeeded in getting many people to buy the goods, which they had strapped around their bodies. There were hawkers selling varieties of food items, books and magazines, tea and coffee, screaming their lungs out in different tones to attract customers. They livened up the otherwise dreary train journey. Despite the heat, the few first-timers on the train chatted in their heavily accented Hindi with the hawkers, who got along with them quite well. Perhaps their years of service in the trains to and from the Northeast had acquainted them with the broken Hindi spoken by their passengers.

After two days and two nights, the train finally halted at the Old Delhi railway station. A whiff of human excreta came in with the morning air. But Rakovei and his friends were too excited to bother about the stench that invaded their nostrils. Anyway, they probably stank as much to others because they had not bathed for two full days and had been sweating profusely. The tap water in the toilet had been a bare trickle, allowing them to just wash their faces and brush their teeth.

As Rakovei stepped onto the platform, Joyson rushed forward with a big smile. He shook hands with Rakovei and helped him with his luggage. Joyson was his second cousin from his father's side and was from

Phyabu village. He had been in Delhi for four years, beginning his studies with a master's programme in the Political Science Department at the University of Delhi. He was now writing his MPhil dissertation. Though related by blood, they had met only a couple of years back, having been kept apart by educational pursuits. When they had last met, Rakovei had just got his matriculation results, and Joyson had come home after finishing his master's degree. When Rakovei expressed a desire to study in Delhi, his parents telephoned Joyson and asked him to let their son stay with him, to which he readily agreed.

'How was the journey?' Joyson asked, wiping the steadily dripping perspiration from his face with a handkerchief. He looked tiny even though he was five and a half feet, an average height for a Naga. But with the tall *Lamais* all around, he seemed to have shrunk.

'It was all right. I didn't know what to expect. This was the first time I have travelled by train.'

'Really? Good for you! Most people find it terrible travelling in the sleeper class at this time because of the heat.'

'Of course, the heat. But we were quite a large group, so we had fun.'

'Are they all first-timers to Delhi?'

'Three of us. The other one said he's been here for two years now doing an undergraduate programme. He was the one who guided us through.'

They took an auto from just outside the station. In

half an hour, they reached Joyson's rented flat in Indira Vihar. He stayed with a friend who had left just two weeks ago after he had got a Probationary Officer's post in the State Bank of Travancore. Joyson's research work had not allowed him to go home for the last two years. Besides, travel always meant incurring extra expenditure. Even though he had a research grant from the university, he could barely make a living out of it because of the high cost of living in the capital city. By nature he was inquisitive and so he kept asking about everybody and everything at home. And the newcomer had to keep up a stream of answers. Just before Rakovei had left for Delhi, he visited Joyson's family and they sent some home-cooked food for him, including smoked meat and dried vegetables. Being unable to reach the village through the phone, Joyson was all the more curious about the people back home.

'How's Uncle Lenny now?' he asked.

'He's improved a lot lately,' Rakovei said. 'He can look after himself now.'

'That's great!' exclaimed Joyson. 'He's not someone who will give up easily. The last time I was home, he was trying to concentrate on his music. How's he doing with that?'

'You know music is his first love. He has composed some beautiful songs, including a very poignant one on the Oinam incident.' Lenny was an enthusiastic guitar player. If it weren't for his mother, who didn't see any future in music, he would have become a musician.

Despite opposition from his family, he tried to start a band, but it failed to take off because of financial reasons. They did not know anyone who had made a successful career out of music, and so it was not surprising that parents couldn't comprehend their children's desire to pursue music as a livelihood. It was seen as a hobby, and everybody could venture into it for fun. To most people, young people who formed a rock band were social rebels who were probably also into drugs. That immediately prompted parents to oppose the idea of their children pursuing music. For Lenny, his physical disability allowed him to indulge his passionate love of music in general and the guitar in particular. A year after his injury, a friend of his managed to buy a rather expensive guitar as a way of cheering him up. Very pleased at the gift, he resumed his music practice and began to compose songs.

It is generally accepted that people from the Northeast seemed to possess considerable musical talent. As children, Rakovei and his cousins had loved listening to Uncle Lenny playing the guitar for them. He encouraged them to strum the instrument, which they happily did whenever they got the chance. The year Rakovei began Class XI, being in the hostel, he learned to play the guitar properly. The hostel owner had provided several items, including guitars, carom boards and chess sets, for the entertainment of the students. The older students even bought decks of cards and played secretly, as it was not permitted. But the guitar was their favourite and everyone would jostle to play it. With just a few notes to learn and strum to the rhythm, it was among the easiest musical instruments to learn. It was also in the hostel that he developed a taste for pop and rock music. When a more experienced guitarist picked up the instrument, the boys joined in to sing along with him—they loved the songs of Mr Big, Bon Jovi, Guns & Roses, Bryan Adams, Def Leppard and the hordes of other Western rock bands that were piling up in each one's cassette collection. They played the songs on the stereo and screamed their lungs out along with the hard rock numbers.

Chapter 14

Life in the city is always in a hurry. One must catch up with it or be left behind. By the early 1990s, as the central government began to throw open its economy, the country's future seemed to have turned a different way. Of course, as always, there were debates over it. After all, India is a democracy, and debates are an essential part of it.

Rakovei's experience of the big city began simultaneously with his life in college. He had enrolled for an undergraduate degree in history at Hans Raj College, University of Delhi. Most of his time was spent in adjusting to the new environment, to a different lot of people with a different mentality, and unbearably hot weather. He visited friends in south Delhi on weekends, but his friends were not keen on coming to his house that often even though it was more spacious. 'It feels odd to have your senior cousin around, we can't have the 'right' fun,' they would say. He knew what they meant. Down south, only people of the same age group stayed together and they would play card games or talk about girls late into the night. Sometimes, they would drink rum or whiskey, but he didn't quite like getting drunk; he would rather stay sober. He had tried alcohol once or twice but had had a bad hangover the next day. It was quite a horrible experience for him, so he tried to avoid alcohol. Also, he didn't want his cousin to find out or his parents, through the grapevine. That would upset them a lot, he thought.

Many parents back home had heard bad news about their children being lost to drink and he didn't want to let his parents suffer the same way. That was why his parents wanted him to stay with Joyson and find a college close to where he lived. And as a way of saying that Joyson had been given this responsibility, even the bank draft for his monthly expenses was sent with his cousin's name neatly written on it. But Rakovei didn't mind. Actually, he liked it that way, because it meant that he didn't have to bother too much with managing the household. All that was required of him was to pursue his studies sincerely. He was happy that classes were taken regularly, as opposed to some of his friends who didn't care if classes were on or not. Many of the colleges functioned like that. Either the lecturers were not sincere about taking classes or the students did not attend classes. It seemed that they went to college out of necessity once in a while, like when they had to fill their exam forms or collect their admit card for the final examination. But they were smart enough not to miss exams lest they be forced to repeat another year. They wouldn't have been able to explain that to their parents.

And yet that was not the case for everyone. There was a fellow from Nagaland living on the floor just above them at Indira Vihar. He had a strange habit of disappearing for days and occasionally brought home friends to party late into the night. Rakovei asked Joyson if he knew the fellow and what he did. Joyson said, 'He's just another boy having the time of his life. This must be his fifth and last year in college. Unfortunately, he is struggling to complete his undergraduate course. Apparently, in the second year he missed some exams because he couldn't get up in the morning. The next year, he made up for his laziness by clearing the repetition of his second year. But the following year, he went on a vacation and didn't come back in time for the exams. I don't know what's going to happen if he doesn't clear the exams this time. His parents probably think he is doing well. I wonder what he has told them. A couple of times, I tried talking to him about the need to get serious about his studies, and each time he said, 'you're right, brother', 'you're right, brother'. But the next day he was off somewhere. Unfortunately, he isn't the only one of our people fooling around and wasting his time. Eventually, they go back home without even completing their course and become social misfits.'

At college, Rakovei had a Kuki friend named Lalboi Haokip in his class. At first, they were both reluctant to befriend each other because they were from Manipur and the Naga-Kuki conflict was still fresh in people's memories. However, a few months later, they began talking. Perhaps their physical appearance set them apart from the rest of their classmates who were mainly from Delhi or other north Indian states and so they got friendly. Over the years, students from the Northeast had made their presence felt, even though they were still a minority on campus. Had he and Lalboi been in Manipur, they would have been termed enemies, but being far away from their homeland they became good buddies. The old neighbourhood relationship of the Nagas and the Kukis suddenly came alive. Lalboi stayed in Malka Ganj, just a few minutes' walk from their college, so Rakovei often went to his friend's place during free periods. Lalboi also visited his house in Indira Vihar. Slowly their talk drifted from college life in Delhi to the situation back home. And inevitably, they ended up lamenting the plight of the people of their home state.

Towards the end of the first year, Lalboi did not show up in college for a few days. Worried that his friend might be sick, Rakovei decided to visit him one day after class. Walking up the stairs of his second floor flat he rang the bell. There was silence. He rang the bell again. A few seconds later, the door knob turned slowly and the door opened a few inches. It was his friend, behind the door, surprised to see a visitor, but he forced a smile and said, 'Hi!'

'What happened to you? Why haven't you been coming to college?' asked Rakovei as he stepped in. On seeing the bandage on Lalboi's right shin and left arm, he was alarmed. 'Did you have an accident?'

'Ah! These local bastards...'

'Why? How?' he cried before Lalboi could finish his sentence.

Taking a deep breath, Lalboi began, 'You know how these people call us 'chinky'? Every time we step out of our house, there is always one group or the other to taunt us, on the street or the market place. Just a couple of days back, I went to buy some vegetables. On my way back, I passed a bunch of boys playing cricket. One of the boys hit the ball and it was coming in my path. Then one of them shouted, *'Oye chinky, ball idhar phek!'* I got suddenly furious and kicked the ball into the ditch. How long can we tolerate them calling us names because of our appearance?' He became agitated as he recounted what had happened. Rakovei could well imagine the scene. Many times he also had been angered when people used indecent terms on the roadside and by-lanes of colonies. But he didn't know what 'chinky' even meant. All he knew was that it was a reference to the way people from the Northeast looked. And yet, he was a little timid, so he would often walk away, pretending to not hear it. However, he knew his friend was more temperamental.

'Were you alone at the time?' he asked.

'Unfortunately, yes. But I wasn't expecting such bad treatment. I thought, what will they do? They'll just come up and confront me and we would have a verbal exchange. But then they came after me with their bats. In defence, I kicked a couple of them down, but I was easily outnumbered.'

'Man, that's terrible! Did you file an FIR?'

'Hah' he said, as though disgusted at the word. 'Do you think the police will do anything? Don't be a fool.'

Rakovei understood what he meant. Just a month ago, a Rongmei Naga from Manipur had been severely beaten by some local boys. After the culprits came to know that he had filed an FIR, they pressurized his landlord, through the local authorities, to force him out. The landlord, a decent man, had to apologize profusely and beg his tenant to leave immediately. Even the landlords were helpless. The poor boy and his friends, instead of getting justice, had to bite another bullet by vacating the flat. Obviously, Lalboi wouldn't want to end up like that. He swallowed the bitter pill and stayed home, nursing his wounds. On hearing the commotion, he said, some elders in the neighbourhood came to his rescue and scolded and chased the kids away. One of those who came to help, a shopkeeper known to him, went and told Thang, his roommate. He was treated at a clinic in the locality and was asked to take complete rest for a week. Thankfully, there were no broken bones, but the bruises on his shin and arm were bad.

'I'm all right now. But for the last two days, I've had a throbbing headache. It wouldn't stop despite the medicine,' Lalboi said.

Rakovei leaned forward to see the mark just behind his friend's left ear, which was still dark blue. 'Ouch! That must really hurt!'

'Yes, it does. A bat hit me there and I went blank. Anyway, I'll recover soon. Don't worry. So tell me, what's happening in college?'

'Nothing, *yaar*. I guess the warmth of their homes is keeping both teachers and students indoors.'

They both burst out laughing. Though considered a premier college of the university, in some ways the functioning was lax. With attendance rarely marked, students also didn't take the classes seriously. They usually skipped classes they thought were boring. Many just hung around the canteen and the open spaces in the campus the whole day, chatting away. Parents thought that their kids were faithfully going to college. Yes, they did come to college, but not to attend classes. The far end of the college joined Bungalow Road, which was lined by bookshops catering to college students, and Kamla Nagar market, a favourite student hangout. That was how college life went.

Later that evening, Rakovei narrated Lalboi's story to Joyson, who was equally infuriated on hearing it and felt sorry for Lalboi. 'These local boys have no decency at all. All they do is provoke people like us who look different,' he said, but he immediately added, 'But everyone is not uncouth. There are many who are really nice.' Perhaps that last sentence was for the sake of the landlord's family who lived downstairs. They had three adult children, two of whom had finished college. Unlike many landlords who would not tolerate the strong smells of dried fish and fermented soya beans emanating from the kitchens of their tenants, this family had no issue whatsoever with the food habits of their tenants. In fact, one of the boys would even come sneaking up whenever Joyson and Rakovei cooked some non-vegetarian food.

'But what does 'chinky' actually mean?' asked Rakovei.

'It's a reference to our physical appearance, the high cheekbones and the narrow eyes. But what's really worrying is that such stereotyping has a deeper underlying meaning, to make us feel that we do not belong in this city.' The philosophical undertone in Joyson's explanation was obvious. Perhaps his years of being in the city had made him read things beyond the surface. True to a research scholar's spirit, he was ready to analyse any given subject. So he went on, 'You must have come across people asking you where you're from, expecting to hear that you're from outside of India, right?'

Rakovei nodded in agreement. 'Just the other day, the shopkeeper at the end of the other lane asked me if I was from Nepal when I went to buy some stuff.' He was quite shocked at the mistaken identity. But Rakovei was also equally surprised to find that the Nepalese, working in various tiny food joints in Delhi or employed as security guards, were very similar to them in physical features. The Nepalis of Manipur were distinct from them, in the sense that they had sharper features.

'That is understandable. And perhaps that old fellow

genuinely wanted to know,' Joyson said. 'But there are those who want to just irritate you by asking such questions, like the youths on the streets. Those are the ones you have to be careful of. Most of these youths are uneducated and ill-behaved. Sometimes they seem like they want to prove that they are locals even though nobody is questioning them. I think there is a deep sense of insecurity among them too because Delhi is largely a city of migrants. On the other hand, when it comes to our experiences, as people from the Northeast, there is a lot to blame on the government's neglect of the region for too long.'

'How's that?'

'We cannot really point a finger at our friends in the university for being so naïve about us. When they were in school hardly anything about the history and culture of the states of the Northeast was taught. You just ask them, they'll tell you. For them, the whole of the Northeast was linked to the rest of the country by a narrow strip of land, and is largely seen as a kind of wasteland, sparsely inhabited by some wild tribes. There might be a mention of the Brahmaputra and a few sketchy remarks about the one-horned rhinoceros found in Kaziranga National Park. Apart from that, there won't be anything much, certainly not about the people. Did our school textbooks have chapters on the culture and history of the Northeast? Or even your history textbooks at college? What mention is there of the Northeast?'

That was something to ponder about, thought Rakovei. He began to reflect on the syllabus that had already been covered so far. He could barely recollect anything about the history of the Northeast in their Indian history books. Was there no history of the region worthy of mention for students of history?

Chapter 15

A city like Delhi could spring surprises at any time, Rakovei concluded. The fact that extremes existed together told a story—from the weather to the people. Based on his experience, he concluded that there were just two kinds of weather in the city, winter and summer. Winter was freezing cold and summer was brutally hot. No wonder the homeless in the streets died during both the seasons. And the people—you could find the kindest souls and also the most intolerant boors in the city. Despite all this, there were many ways to get hooked to Delhi and fall for its attractions.

It was a hot afternoon. Rakovei and Joyson were riding on a rickshaw to Sir Shankar Lal Hall in the university campus for the Naga Students' Union's Freshers' Meet, an annual programme organized to welcome students from different Naga tribes who had come to study in the capital city. Just as they stopped at the traffic light, a loud Royal Enfield pulled up next to them. Rakovei turned to see who was riding it. To his astonishment, an army man in an olive green uniform, with the three-headed lion insignia neatly pinned on each shoulder, was proudly holding the bike's handles. The Royal Enfield had the same colours as his uniform, unlike the usual black ones Rakovei had seen. His turban was also military green, and a pistol was strapped to his hip. With his well-oiled beard and twirled mustache, the well-built Sikh major was a figure that would command respect among his comrades. Rakovei craned his neck to see who was guarding the army man, but there was no one! The major was out on the road, riding his bike alone! For the first time in his life, Rakovei came face to face with a major without a platoon of soldiers surrounding him. He blinked in disbelief. Joyson noticed his reaction. 'Eh! What are you doing? You don't look at people like that. Stop staring,' he admonished. Rakovei looked away at once, a little embarrassed. He felt the major was also turning towards him. 'Stupid...what have you done,' he scolded himself.

Throughout the NSUD function, Rakovei thought about the major at the traffic light and couldn't concentrate on the day's events. Every time a person stepped on the podium, Rakovei saw the face of the major. How could a soldier of his rank expose himself to the public? Or was he an impersonator trying to live his dream of military glory? No, that couldn't be true, he thought. Only a child would pretend, not an adult.

Later that evening, when he was on the small balcony facing the main lane, Joyson's voice invaded his thoughts. 'What happened? You looked so melancholic today.'

'It's nothing,' he said. 'It's just that I thought today's programme was a little boring.'

'Really? I thought it was one of the best NSUD Freshers' Meets I've attended in the last few years.'

Oh, no! What have I said, Rakovei thought. He had uttered the words without thinking. Should he speak about what was really on his mind? Would his cousin find it silly and laugh at him? Would he really understand? He finally spoke. 'Joyson, do you think the Major on the motorcycle at the traffic light we saw this morning was a real army major?'

'Of course, he was real. Why would somebody pretend to be a soldier on the road while he was alone? He wasn't acting in a movie. Did you see any film crew around?' He laughed at the last statement.

'But he was alone. No bodyguards...'

'This is not Manipur or Nagaland or the Northeast!' Joyson interjected, half laughing, half serious.

'What do you mean?'

'You still have so much to learn about the harsh conditions faced by our people. It's AFSPA that makes our side of the country different from this side.'

'Really?'

He had heard of AFSPA, the Armed Forces Special Powers Act of 1958, but had never given it much thought. Joyson explained that it was first promulgated to suppress the Naga uprising in the declared 'disturbed areas' of Assam and the Union Territory of Manipur by empowering the Indian armed forces, and now extended to most parts of the Northeastern region. These 'special powers' gave the right, not just to the commissioned but even the non-commissioned army personnel to arrest, detain, shoot or even kill on mere suspicion and without having to explain their actions and without being prosecuted. No wonder he had always seen the army personnel as all-powerful, Rakovei thought.

He had seen Joyson getting agitated when this topic came up in discussions with his friends, as though something had pierced his soul. Certainly, Joyson had done a good deal of research on the subject, so he knew what he was talking about. Rakovei had frequently browsed his cousin's collection of books on the shelf near the study table. He remembered some of the titles now—Asoso Yunuo's *The Rising Nagas*, Nirmal Nebidon's *Nagaland: The Night of the Guerillas* and Luingam Luithui & Nandita Haksar's *Nagaland File: A Question of Human Rights.* He had tried reading *The Rising Nagas* because Joyson had told him that that the author was one of their own people called Kosa, literally meaning 'cat', the name by which Asoso Yunuo was popularly known in the community. He was a well-known character. Stories were told of his shrewdness and cleverness. Supposedly, even as a child he was very mischievous. He was so tiny that he could even crawl into the *houphe*, the small chicken coop traditionally woven with split bamboo for one hen and its chicks, and hide while his parents searched frantically for him.

'Is AFSPA a component of your research?' Rakovei

once asked him, out of curiosity, for he seemed to know quite a lot.

'I wanted to work on the ill-effects of AFSPA, but my supervisor didn't allow me to do so because he thinks I get too emotional when it comes to that topic.' He paused and then said, 'But we cannot be less sensitive when we have seen how it violates our right to live with dignity.'

Rakovei knew that the pronoun 'we' was intended to include him too. And he didn't mind. As his cousin spoke, he recalled the bitter memories of Operation Bluebird. Now he understood why the army was so powerful and acted without any fear. Without a law to penalize them, they had all the power to act mercilessly. He wondered if the families who had suffered the loss of their dear ones at the hands of the army would ever find justice.

The afternoon slowly gave way to evening. Somewhere in the western sky the sun was sinking down. But where the two cousins lived, the surrounding tall buildings obstructed the view. Besides, the murky Delhi sky did not allow the movement of the sun during the day or the moon at night to be seen clearly. In the first few months, Rakovei had complained that he could not see the stars at night. The few times he went up to the terrace to look at the heavenly bodies in the hope of easing his homesickness, he had been unlucky. Back home, most nights the stars would shine bright, even though the moon would make its timely disappearance.

But as time went by, he forgot to look up at the sky. Anyway, it was always a useless effort. The noisy fan inside the room attracted his attention. The first few nights he could not sleep because of the heat and the noise of the fan. A couple of times he woke up in the middle of the night and wondered if it was raining, only to realize that he was in Delhi and it was only the sound of the fan. It sounded like rain falling on the tin roofs of houses back home. However, like everyone else, he too eventually got used to life in Delhi. He still found it terrible travelling on city buses, whether they were the government-owned DTC buses or the privately-run Blue Line buses. But taking buses was the only means for him to visit his friends in south Delhi because taking autos was too expensive and taxis were not even to be thought of on the kind of allowance his parents sent him each month. He felt terribly tired every time he got off a bus. He imagined pollution invading his poor heart. Surprisingly, however, people from different parts of the country flocked to Delhi and they loved it. After all, life was bustling in the city. And slowly Rakovei began to analyse things, joining different pieces of realization to form a complete whole. In Delhi, there were no military convoys storming down the roads. There were no foot soldiers patrolling the locality. There were no search operations. Then, he thought, why wouldn't people love Delhi?

There were other reasons why the city attracted more and more young people every year. The availability of universities that provided quality education was one of the top reasons. The numbers of students from the Northeast enrolling in different undergraduate programmes began to rise by the year. In recent years, they had become quite a presence in all the central universities in the capital. There was a time when the farthest places most parents were willing to send their children were Shillong and Guwahati. Now they were willing to send their children across the country in search of better education, the conditions of education at home having deteriorated drastically in recent times. Most young people had lost faith in the education system in their home states. It was unfortunate that students from states like Manipur had to face additional stress because of ethnic violence. Even though the dust of violence seemed to have settled down, there were apprehensions in every mind. Besides, for a state that was home to a conglomeration of ethnic groups, tension always persisted in the air. The polarization of these groups had been sharpened by the emergence of insurgent groups that vowed to fight for the rights of each group. Therefore, the state continued to remain a 'disturbed area' for various reasons.

Chapter 16

As his second-year final examination was about to start, some of Rakovei's friends asked him if he would be going home for the summer so that they could book tickets in advance. But for once he was undecided. The thought of the train trip by sleeper class wasn't appealing. Yet his parents didn't want him to travel alone while all his friends travelled by sleeper class. He couldn't claim to be richer than his friends. He still remembered how the journey felt. May usually was the hottest and driest month in Delhi, as also in other parts of north India. And to travel by train, particularly by sleeper class, wasn't enjoyable. But he didn't think of all this last year. He was quite homesick then, having been away from home for almost a whole year. He didn't think twice about going home then. And his friends felt the same. Though excited in the beginning, later they all felt the journey by the Brahmaputra Mail was too long. To make matters worse, the train reached Dimapur station at midnight. So they stayed at the station, half asleep and half awake, breathing in the stink of the excreta emanating from the rail tracks as they waited for dawn. The fact that they couldn't bathe for two days on the train made things worse. Their clothes reeked of sweat. Had they reached a bit earlier, they would have found a hotel to stay in, but because they arrived at midnight, they had to stay out all night at the railway station. Besides, Dimapur was no better in terms of weather—it was hot and humid. Even at night, the humidity persisted.

As soon as it was dawn, they hurried to the taxi station. Finding a taxi, they loaded their baggage and the vehicle sped off. A few minutes later, they hit the NH 39. Rakovei turned to his good buddy Manikho. 'Do you think the road has shrunk?'

Manikho burst out laughing, but then in order not to upset Rakovei he stopped and asked, 'Why do you say that?'

'Don't you think the highway has become smaller since the last time we saw it?'

'Come on, do you really think that? Maybe you need some more sleep.'

'I sure do,' he muttered, as he yawned. He felt foolish asking the question. And yet he couldn't believe the tarred highway was barely broad enough to let two vehicles pass. He thought how the roads in Delhi were two or three lanes on each side. Perhaps, being used to seeing the broad roads in the city had made the highway in this part of the world seem even smaller. Though the road was a national highway, without even a road divider, it looked more like a single-lane driveway in some of the colonies in the city. But it was amazing how the taxi driver zoomed at top speed despite the hairpin bends and curves. Did he possess a sixth sense that warned him of an approaching vehicle from the opposite direction so that he could drive even faster?

Anyway, it was a wonderful vacation. He couldn't complain about it. Being at home with his parents was reason enough to be happy. And to see the two younger ones who had grown tremendously in just a year was a joy. Chasü was already in Class III and Veine in Class I. They screamed with joy when they saw him, as though he had come from a different planet or was appearing after a lifetime. For them Rakovei was a hero. His parents treated him as an adult and they, particularly his mother, wouldn't stop asking about his experiences in the big city. Through his narrative they also lived the city life. They occasionally talked over the phone, but it was a different experience talking face to face.

Unfortunately, the summer vacation was soon over and he had to endure the much-dreaded train journey. Of course, he didn't tell that part of the story to his family. They would be displeased, he thought. Soon the band of friends met and headed to the city they had pledged to come back to. Like everyone, he had also stuffed lots of homemade items, including smoked meat and dry vegetables, into his luggage.

'I'm not sure if I should go home this time,' Rakovei said to Joyson one day over lunch. 'Some of my friends wanted to know my plans so that they could book the train tickets. But I also feel that spending almost two months of summer vacation in Delhi may be a bit too boring.' His parents had left it to him to decide whether to come home or not.

'You should experience the Delhi summer!' his cousin said in jest. 'But seriously, what will you do even if you go home? It would be much more useful staying here. You could read some books or attend a summer camp.' Joyson was regarded even among his peers as the most serious and dedicated when it came to studies. He often encouraged those younger to him, even Rakovei's friends whenever they visited, to read books, saying there was only something to be gained and nothing to lose. He was now registered in a PhD programme and had been busy visiting libraries and writing papers. Being mostly engaged with books and not the type to engage in sports, he appeared to have put on some weight lately, making him rounder in the middle. Though he had been in Delhi for some years, he hadn't got used to the sweat dripping down, and his trademark white handkerchief was always in his left hand to wipe off perspiration. Wiping his forehead and neck with it had become a habit, even in winter. He was a pragmatist at heart and always weighed something in his mind before undertaking it. The last time he went home was the previous October, but he made it part of his research project to collect some data.

The next day, Joyson came home with something that he thought would interest his younger cousin.

'I've got something you can consider doing during your vacation.'

Rakovei was not sure how to respond. He didn't want to disappoint his cousin. Hoping that it would be something worth devoting his time to, he said, 'Really? What is it?'

'The Naga People's Movement for Human Rights has come up with a proposal to commemorate the Oinam incident on 9 July this year. A few other civil rights organizations operating in the city have encouraged it to organize a programme and most likely it will do so. I thought you could be a volunteer for the programme.'

Joyson had been an active member of the Delhi chapter of NPMHR for some time. He had been asked to be its convener the previous year, but had declined the request, saying his hands were full and that he would be willing to help whenever needed, but not as a core member. Earlier that morning, he told Rakovei that he was going to a meeting of some senior Nagas in the city with NPMHR.

'Hmm...What sort of work is it?'

'There aren't any concrete plans as of now, but it won't take up too much of your time, don't worry. You can come along with me the next time they call a meeting. I've been asked to speak on how people were affected during Operation Bluebird. You said you were also in the village at that time. How did you feel then?'

Rakovei felt a bit odd to be asked because no one had ever asked him about that time. It was strange that even the two of them had not talked much about the incident beyond the effects on Uncle Lenny. They kept quiet about it as a kind of shared understanding. Perhaps the silence was part of an extended condolence for the victims of the military operation. Suddenly he became melancholic at the thought of it. 'It was a horrifying experience and I also felt terribly betrayed.'

Joyson looked at Rakovei in some alarm. He didn't understand what his young cousin had just said. Betrayed by whom? Just as he was about to ask, Rakovei intercepted his thought and explained, 'For a long time I had dreamed of becoming an army officer. I used to admire the men in their olive green camouflage uniforms riding in the convoy of military trucks, coloured like their uniform. I guess it was part of a child's dream, of wanting to hold an automatic rifle or an AK-47. I never knew they were such brutal soldiers, torturing innocent people. What I saw them do to the villagers was unforgivable. Their torture left people like my uncle impaired for life. That was the biggest blow to my first dream in life. Since then my admiration for them has turned into hate. Every time I see them patrol on the road or see their convoy rolling down the highway, something bitter grows inside me. I don't see the glamour in them anymore.'

After his second-year final exam, Rakovei accompanied Joyson to a couple of the NPMHR meetings and learned that the organization planned to make the Oinam incident a focal point of the next issue of their journal. The NPMHR had long campaigned against human rights violations by the Indian armed forces in Naga areas. As volunteers, students like Rakovei were asked to distribute brochures to different student bodies, not just within the sub-units of the Naga Students' Union, but also to like-minded organizations in the city. But since this was not a daily task, on some evenings he went out to play football with friends and came back exhausted. During the day, kept indoors because of the heat, he read some novels that he had picked up from the roadside bookstalls or bought at the Sunday second-hand book market at Daryaganj. Some of the books were part of Joyson's collection. Of late, he had got hooked to Western spaghetti novels and had decided that Louis L'Amour was his favourite author. He also immensely enjoyed Mario Puzo's mafia novels.

When 9 July, the day of commemoration, finally dawned, he was satisfied at the turnout. What touched him particularly was that many non-Nagas came to show their solidarity on the issue, some of whom even took to the stage to affirm their support for the struggle for justice. Two young boys sang the poignant song 'Oinam, Oh Oinam', written by the Naga theologian Rev. Dr. Wati Aier, which by now had become the theme song of the incident.

When it was Joyson's turn to speak, Rakovei sneaked up to the front of the gathering, hoping to hear his cousin better. With a few words of profuse apology to the gathering that he would have to be brief because of time, he took a deep breath and began.

'Eight years ago, on 9 July 1987, an incident occurred in the sleepy village of Oinam in Senapati District of Manipur that changed the course of history of the people in the region. On that day, the NSCN cadres attacked the Assam Rifles post at Oinam, killing nine soldiers, injuring a few, and sparing the rest by locking them up in their mess hall. They fled with all the arms and ammunition stocked in the camp. It was a total humiliation for the Assam Rifles who prided themselves for their training in the Counter-Insurgency Jungle Warfare School in Mizoram. What immediately followed, therefore, was the launch of Operation Bluebird by the Assam Rifles, aided by several Indian armed forces operating in the region, on the pretext of recovering the arms and ammunition looted by the Naga undergrounds. More than thirty villages in and around Oinam were cordoned off immediately and indefinite curfew was enforced, which lasted for more than three months. Villagers could not even go into their fields to drive away wayward cattle. Innocent people were indiscriminately tortured without reason, leaving many of them maimed to this day. In all, twenty-seven men from different villages were killed by the Indian armed forces, either by being directly shot, tortured or because of electric shocks. Many were physically maimed for life and many continue to suffer chronic illnesses related to torture. In one of the most shameful acts, the soldiers forced a woman in Oinam Hill village to give birth in full public view. After more than three months, the

Assam Rifles called off Operation Bluebird without having achieved their mission, that is, to recover the lost weapons. All they left behind were the wounds, mental, psychological and physical, on the innocent people. The pain they endured is still fresh in their memories, even to this day.'

He paused to let the audience mull over the gravity of his words. Then he resumed, 'Today, as we commemorate the Oinam incident, let us introspect about the kinds of laws that are in place in the country. NPMHR has been a major campaigner against the excessive powers invested in the Indian armed forces through the AFSPA in most parts of the Northeast. But it could do nothing against the empowered military forces in the declared 'disturbed areas'. We should understand that the AFSPA grants special powers to any member of the armed forces to arrest, detain, shoot or kill even on mere suspicion. I stress 'any' because the power is given even to non-commissioned officers, that is, the lowest ranking armed personnel. No legal action can be taken against them. It is because of this Act that the Indian armed forces are able to operate without fear of human rights violation because they have guaranteed protection. India is a signatory to the UN Declaration of Human Rights, but has been blind and deaf to the atrocities committed by the Assam Rifles during Operation Bluebird. A democratic nation that treats a section of its people, no matter how tiny they are, with harshness, cannot claim to stand for the people, by the people and for the people. Therefore, I call upon the gathering today to condemn the Act that violates the rights of the citizens of the country. Instead of building a country on mutual respect and dignity, AFSPA only alienates and embitters the minds and hearts of the people. Thank you.'

There was applause as Joyson left the podium. Rakovei smiled while his eyes turned wet with unshed tears. Silently he wiped his tears away with his handkerchief.

Boy, that was quite something, Rakovei thought about the summer vacation that just went by. He wasn't thinking so much of the voluntary summer internship with NPMHR but of Awon. When he met her for the first time, he felt nervous and giddy. They met in an ordinary way. He was waiting to give directions to people attending the NPMHR meeting being held at the secretary's house. Joyson had said that some people might not be able to find their way in, and had asked him to wait at a particular spot for some time and direct the people to the house. The lane was narrow, and he stood at the entry point so that people would not miss it. He was glad there was a little shade in the corner where he could escape the worst of Delhi's fearsome summer heat.

'Excuse me, is this the way to Jerry's house?'

Two girls stood before him. Both wore light-coloured tops and blue jeans. From their clothes he would have concluded they were twins. The one who spoke to him had her hair trimmed in a fringe and wore gold-rimmed spectacles. Her name was Awon, as he learned later. The other girl was Shonrin, and she had a neatly tied ponytail. Rakovei decided that Awon was the more attractive of the two, for she had a thoughtful look, which he found enchanting.

'Yes. This way please. The place is the third on the right on the second floor.'

He blushed. He quickly covered his face with his handkerchief, pretending to wipe away perspiration. Strange, he thought later, why was he nervous? It wasn't the first time that he had met beautiful girls. He had fallen for a few girls before, though most of these crushes were secret. A couple of times when he had come to know that they were girlfriends of guys he knew, he felt jealous. But he had not had the guts to propose to a girl so far. He prayed that this latest encounter would lead to something. The two girls had also volunteered for the same programme as him. After attending a few of these meetings, they started talking. But he realized that Awon avoided him. He wondered why. It was only many months later, when they went on their first date that she confessed that she had liked him from the first instance and that made her a bit uncomfortable.

'You mean you were trying to avoid me because you liked me?' Rakovei asked.

'I didn't know how to handle the situation or my

feelings,' she said, turning aside, blushing a little and unable to to look face to face with him.

'Hmm...interesting.'

'What is?'

'I mean avoiding someone because you like the person! Ha ha...'

She gave him a withering look.

'Sorry, I didn't mean to...' he said, turning serious, but not sure if he should say anything more.

'It's okay,' she said, recovering her sense of humour. 'I know it's funny, but what to do? That's the way I am.'

He wasn't sure if she has spoken in self-defence. He decided to admit his weakness too. 'Actually, I also had a funny feeling when I first met you.'

'I know. You blushed!' she laughed.

'You saw?'

'Of course. Anybody could see it.'

'Come on, you're kidding.'

'No way. Shonrin and I giggled about it the whole evening. You were the first guy who had blushed in front of me!'

'Come on...' Now it was his turn to be laughed at.

Nevertheless, they had a good time together that afternoon. Awon was pursuing her BA (Hons) in English from Jesus and Mary College. Ever since they became friendly, he began to visit his friends in south Delhi more frequently. His friends pulled his leg initially about his newfound love, but soon the novelty wore off and the matter was forgotten. They had been going steady for about a year when he discovered that her father was a big shot in the underground movement. He didn't know how to react to the news.

'Why didn't you tell me your father is an underground?' He wasn't sure if he had used the right term. Usually they were referred to as 'national workers' or 'freedom fighters' with a sense of pride.

'Why? Does it matter?' Her sudden defensiveness made him wonder if he had asked the wrong question.

'No...just that...I was just asking.'

'Why can't people like me live a normal life?' It was a rhetorical question and he didn't know how to react to it. 'Every time someone finds out about our family, they start avoiding us. I don't know why. It's been almost seven years since I last saw my father, and that too for only a few days. It feels awkward to meet him when he comes. He is more like a guest. We all grew up without our father. Sometimes it pains me to see how my mother has to manage everything on her own. I'm not trying to praise my mother, but no ordinary woman would have done what she has done for us.'

Awon's story reminded him of the many families he knew from his own village. It chilled him to think that many of those children would not get to see their fathers come home.

Chapter 17

There are moments in life when you look back and regret not doing what you could or should have done. It was a pleasant afternoon in November and Rakovei was relaxing on his bed, which was laid on the floor. He had just come back from college and was enjoying the silence of the room. Just then, he heard the landlady shouting his name, saying there was a phone call from home. Oh no, why did they call, he thought, didn't I tell them I would call when needed. But as he quickly put on his t-shirt and went down the stairs, it struck him that it had been several weeks since he had last called home. He disliked going inside the landlady's house to receive calls because he felt he was invading their privacy. The phone was located in an interior room, which meant he had to make his way past all the other rooms and be exposed to their private life. Being the ground floor, it was usually dingy and he hated the smell emanating from their rooms. But they were nice enough to Rakovei and Joyson and always insisted that they could take calls from their families at any time. 'You stay so far away from home, don't hesitate to tell your parents to call whenever they want, we understand,' they would say.

As he entered their house, however, he realized it must be an urgent matter. He said a quick prayer that it not be bad news. 'Hello!' he said.

'Rakovei, how are you?' It was his father. It was usually his mother first on the line, but his father surprised him today.

'I'm well. How's everyone at home?'

'We're all fine. Can you call home later when you're free?'

'What happened?'

'Don't panic,' his father said. 'It's just that I thought it may be more appropriate for you to talk from a PCO.'

'All right. I'll call right away.' As he hung up the phone, his heart was pounding so loudly that he thought others could hear it.

'Are you done so soon? Or did the line get cut?' the landlady asked, surprised that the call had lasted for just half a minute.

He was a bit embarrassed that the conversation with his parents had been so brief. 'Yes, it is all done. It was just a quick conversation. Thank you.'

He ran up the stairs, picked up his wallet, and went out again to the market to call his parents. He didn't want to wait. Joyson was at the Nehru Memorial Library, so Rakovei latched the door and ran down to the PCO on the main road. As he nervously dialed his home number, he realized that he was sweating inside the small one-person-at-a-time phone booth. When he called out to the fellow at the counter to switch on the tiny fan inside the booth, the man gave him a strange look. Suddenly it struck him that it was November, and so he smiled back. After redialing the number a few times, he finally got through.

'Hello!' It was his mother's voice at the end of the line. It was always nicer when his mother picked up the phone.

'How are you, *pfü*?'

'We are all doing well. How's everything with you?'

'Very good.'

'We were hoping you would call for the last few weeks. But since you didn't, we called. Did your *puo* tell you the news?'

'No. What is it, *pfü*?' His anxiety grew and his heart raced. He dreaded hearing bad news from home.

'Rakovei, your grandmother, Toukhue, passed away last week. We know you might be upset that we didn't inform you earlier, but...'

Rakovei was stunned at first, but then the tears came unbidden. His mother tried to console him. Between sobs, he asked how Grandmother had died.

Grandmother was always a strong woman, with a large heart. There was no sign of illness. It was just old age. Even in death she didn't bother anyone. She slept through the night and then went peacefully to her eternal sleep.

Back in his room, Rakovei was overcome by

memories of his beloved grandmother and tears rolled down his cheeks afresh. He was always her favourite grandchild. Though he didn't stay in the village with her all the time, he knew that she had a soft spot for him. She stored many goodies for him, which she gave him when he visited the village. Now when he went to the village, there would be a huge empty feeling. Who would tell them stories now? He experienced a deep sadness. If only he had gone home for the summer, he would have had the chance to meet her for the last time and say goodbye. But then he didn't know her time was at hand. Such was death. It came silently and without warning. And yet, it was so certain, as certain as the night. One could only hope that it would not come while one was still young. Grandmother had lived her life, a full life. There wouldn't be any regrets for her.

When Joyson came back, he found the house unusually quiet and Rakovei lost in thought. Seeing Rakovei's puffy eyes, he asked, 'What happened?'

'My parents called earlier today and told me that my grandmother Toukhue died a few days ago,' he said, his voice choking.

'Oh no! I'm so sorry to hear that. How did she die? Was she ill?'

'No. She was found dead on her bed.'

'Hmm...death...' Joyson said. 'It's something we cannot help. In a way, it's good that she died that way, I mean, without sickness. We should not regret her passing, except that we stay so far from home and could not attend the funeral.'

'Yeah, that's the only thing on my mind now. If only I had gone home in the summer.'

'No, no...You have to be strong for her sake. We'll all see her again someday soon.'

Yes, I must be strong for her sake, he said to himself.

A month later, in the second week of December, the cousins received some more disconcerting news. This time it hit Joyson harder. In a factional fight between the IM and the K, Ngaolounü, one of his cousins from his mother's side, had been killed. The encounter, which took place on the outskirts of Dimapur town, claimed eleven lives, seven from the IM and four from the K. Since their split in 1988, the men who had once been brothers-in-arms had turned bitter foes, and frequent violent encounters between them were reported from different locations. The wounds within the large Naga family deepened with each fight. Ngaolounü had long been with the NSCN and had regretted it deeply when the breakup occurred. He had once visited Delhi and Joyson had tried his best to convince him to retire from the underground life, arguing that the leaders had squandered the people's future in favour of their own vested interests. Ngaolounü at that time had been vehemently opposed to his cousin's stance, being a strong nationalist from the start. But lately he seemed to have come around to accepting Joyson's point of view. The two cousins had spoken at length over the phone about two months ago. After that Joyson told Rakovei that his cousin might be quitting the underground life, which was a great relief to him. But sadly it was not to be. Joyson wept bitterly.

A few days later, Rakovei took the opportunity to voice some thoughts that had perturbed him over the year. When it came to Naga nationalism, Joyson had a different stance, which intrigued Rakovei. He remembered in particular the time when Joyson and Ngaolounü had argued over it. He had been a silent spectator then, trying to understand the 'big talk'. But he couldn't understand Joyson's scepticism about the future of Naga nationalism. He had participated in the conversations when Joyson and his friends would discuss everything under the sky. He loved those talks because they were lighthearted and harmless. But he was silent when the talk turned political.

So, on a chilly morning as they were having breakfast, sitting in bed under a Moreh blanket, he asked, 'Do you think these factional fights will ever end?'

'I'm not an optimist here,' Joyson said, taking a big bite of the bread omelette and gulping a mouthful of tea. 'What are the chances that it will end when we have left each other hungry for vengeance? I tell you, Nagas will go down with it. And don't think that it is something that started in 1988, even though most people seem to refer to that point, because there have been more killings among Nagas since that time. We have been killing each other since the beginning of the armed struggle for freedom. Sometimes I feel the 'warrior spirit' in us has driven out our sanity.'

'What makes you think so?'

'We have had factional killings for what seems like forever.'

He believed that most of the Naga intellectuals in the city were strongly against his point of view. This was because they were aligned to a particular faction, even though they would not admit it.

'If the undergrounds hear me say these kinds of things, they will send a bullet after me, ha ha...' His laughter was tinged with sarcasm. 'Do you know who the first big victim of factionalism was? It was T. Sakhrie. He was an erudite young fellow, and a relative of A.Z. Phizo, the acknowledged father of Naga nationalism. He was the able secretary of the NNC. He was shot to death for daring to suggest that the Nagas should negotiate with the Government of India. At that time, the Nagas were led by the more radical group, which refused to have anything to do with India. And everyone was carried away by their words. After Jawaharlal Nehru was humiliated by the Nagas when he visited Kohima, the Indian armed forces were sent immediately to crush the Naga movement. Then blood and tears followed.'

Joyson paused briefly as if to signal a transition in his recital of Naga history. Draining his cup, he continued, 'I'm sure at that time our people thought 'independence' would come the 'next day'. But the 'next day' refused to dawn and we are still waiting for it even today. India knew fully well that not everyone agreed with the NNC stance—to achieve sovereignty through armed struggle. It craftily struck a deal with the moderate Nagas and created the state of Nagaland under the Constitution of India in 1963. The NNC continued to keep their torch burning in the jungles. But a new adversary was created, that is, those who had joined hands to form the new state, and the NNC began to target them. Then came another big blow in 1975 when the Shillong Accord was signed by a section of the NNC who agreed to surrender and lay down arms. The members who surrendered were kept in transition camps called peace camps. And the numbers of their detractors increased. Surely and slowly, the Naga undergrounds turned their attention from fighting the Indian army to hunting down and killing those they considered to be the 'betrayers' of the cause. In 1980, the NSCN was formed to denounce both the Shillong Accord and the NNC leaders, including Phizo, who was still busy trying to garner support in the UK and from the West, for not denouncing the Shillong Accord. The NSCN vowed to carry the mantle of hope for the Naga people. But as in the past, ideological differences arose, and the NSCN split in 1988 into NSCN-IM and NSCN-K, with each projecting itself as the 'true' bearer of the torch of Naga nationalism. And the infighting continues, Naga against Naga.'

'But I don't think the people back home see it that

way. We were always told that the IM is the original organization and the K is the breakaway group,' said Rakovei.

'Our people back home have no choice but to take only what is given to them. And they seem happy with the situation. Ideologically, however, there is no room for fair debate in our society. The majority view always triumphs. The less popular opinion is always dismissed. That's why the factions try to assert their authority by exterminating each other. Allegiance to the factions varies from region to region among the Nagas, depending on which group dominates the region. Wherever the IM group dominates, they sell their version of the story about why the split happened and paint the K group as black, even going to the extent of calling Khaplang 'Lucifer'. In the same way, the K group sells their version of the story in the regions where they dominate with equal vigour and paint the IM as debased. Our people are very gullible. The saying 'ignorance is bliss' can be rightly applied to our folks. Do the people know the real story? What really happened in the jungles of Burma? That's a secret that we may never know.'

'Is there any chance of compromise between the groups? After all, the goal is more or less the same,' said Rakovei.

'Call me a sceptic, but I don't see much hope if the leaders continue to stick to their current stance. To most people, the two factions of NSCN seem to be the only active groups. But the old NNC is also still in existence, even though its leader Adino, Phizo's daughter, commands the group from faraway England. I don't see them sitting down at a table for talks when they are busy tracking each other down. Each one is trying to put a bullet into the other's heart. They have hidden daggers, ready to slit each other's throat. Whether we like it or not, the game has been played to give India the advantage, and she's having the last laugh. India is much more than what our people think. We're trapped in our own tiny world, like the proverbial frog that thinks the pond in which it lives is the whole world. Our world is drying up. Will these undergrounds learn that they have been pitted against each other? Will they ever realize that they have been played with and been made fools of? Technically, India washed its hand of the whole affair after the creation of Nagaland. They consider the Naga problem solved. They dismiss sporadic incidents of violence here and there as 'law and order' problems. And nor do I think they are wrong. From their perspective, the Nagas are like stubborn children demanding unreasonably expensive and unaffordable things. India cannot easily give in to the demands of the Nagas and forget other groups demanding the same. They know there's a lot at stake here.'

Joyson's analysis of the Naga political problem was radically different from what Rakovei had always thought. Being completely out of depth in his understanding of things, he let his cousin continue.

'The sooner the underground groups understand that these killings are hurting the larger Naga society, the more hope we have for a better future. Every time a family loses a son or a daughter to these factional wars, the numbers of people seeking vengeance increases. How many Nagas will be sacrificed in the name of the nation? I wonder if the NSCN really understands what it claims to stand for. While their motto may be 'Nagaland for Christ', they seem to be on a killing spree. What does Christ stand for? Behind the façade of Christianity, the most horrible things are being done. It's a shame. If they are really Christians as they claim to be, they ought to love each other and not kill. They ought to heal wounds and not inflict pain. Instead, with their murderous hearts, they are labelling each other Judases and trying to kill one another. But do they know that Jesus gave Judas enough time to repent? They ought to first remember what the Bible says about judging people—'Why do you look at the speck of sawdust in your brother's eye and pay no attention to the plank in your own eye?'

Joyson tried to end his long disquisition on a humorous note. 'Don't let anybody know what I just said. I'll be done for the very next day!' They both burst out laughing, but the next moment fell silent. They knew the seriousness of the matter.

Joyson excused himself and went to the toilet. Still wrapped in the soft blanket, Rakovei began to imagine the whole Naga imbroglio as the plot of a Mario Puzo novel in which rival mafia families conspire to destroy each other to take over the businesses of the city or town. Had the Nagas gone down the same road? Where would all the factional killings lead their society? He didn't want to believe all that Joyson had just said, but in his heart he knew that what Joyson said was true.

Chapter 18

The last two decades of the twentieth century saw many changes in Naga society. For most people, it was adjusting to these new changes that defined their lives and also inspired the stories they told each other.

The arrival of the new millennium did not usher in any significant positive change, at least on the political front. Hopes of the birth of a Naga nation were slowly fading away, seeming like a delusion. The generation who lived to see the dawn of the new millennium was a betrayed generation. For the first generation, the dream of a sovereign nation had been so strong that they had willingly died with dignity in the struggle to achieve it. But now was there anything worth dying for? With the Indo-Naga political conflict pervading every sphere of life, it had become difficult to think about anything independent of it. Everything had a political undertone.

A year after Rakovei graduated, news of the ceasefire agreement between the NSCN-IM, the dominant Naga underground group, and the Government of India, rekindled hope for an amicable solution to the protracted conflict. He recalled the eager anticipation of his people who had long awaited peace in their land, longed for the sound of gunfire to cease, and prayed for mothers to stop weeping for their dead children whose bodies were brought home from some distant land. The blue Naga flag, with its tricolour stripes and star, flew proudly in every corner of Nagalim, the Naga inhabited areas, as though to welcome the agreement between the long-standing foes. Disregarding the existence of other factions among the underground groups, notably the NSCN-K, the Naga people pinned their hopes on the steps taken by the IM group and showed their support for an honourable solution between the Nagas and the Government of India.

However, a year later, the NSCN-K, not to be outdone, also concluded a ceasefire agreement with the Government of India. There were also the NNC (A) and its splintered twin, the FGN, but they had been lying low, like badly wounded warriors with little hope to return to the battlefield.

A few years after the signing of the ceasefire agreement, 'high-level' official talks were held in some third-party countries, mainly Thailand and Holland. This led to ever-increasing hope. In January 2003, when the NSCN leaders Isak Chishi Swu and Thuingaleng Muivah agreed to visit Delhi at the invitation of the Prime Minister of India, Atal Bihari Vajpayee, there were even more inflated hopes. This jubilant optimism was clearly seen when Naga students in Delhi swarmed the Indira Gandhi International Airport to welcome the two leaders, with smiles on their faces and the Naga flag in their hands. For once, photographs of India's most stubborn insurgent groups appeared on the front pages of the national dailies. The media suddenly showed a keen interest in the problems of the Northeast. Back home, the Naga people—spread across Nagaland, Manipur and parts of Assam and Arunachal Pradesh—closely followed the news of the negotiation between India and the Naga leaders.

Rakovei had a vivid memory of the day when the two leaders stepped out of the airport. It was a very cold January day, but everyone braved the chill and went to the airport. It was a historic moment for him and for many others like him. The crowd consisted mostly of students from different universities in the city, but there were also many like him, young working people.

He had joined the banking sector as a probationary officer at the State Bank of Hyderabad after a few failed attempts at cracking the UPSC examinations. The banking sector was not his first choice, but his failure to secure a government job left him with no choice. Besides, there was pressure from his parents to find a job and support the family. After two years of being posted in different cities during his training period, he decided that he had a strange liking for Delhi, despite the pollution and the extreme weather. When he gave Delhi as his first option for his posting after completing his training, he didn't expect much. He was surprised when he got it and joined his office with some excitement. He had completed a year when the news came that the two Naga leaders would finally come to Delhi after more than three decades of self-imposed exile for political negotiation with Indian leaders.

Time seemed to go by so fast, thought Rakovei. It was the winter of 2008, just another Sunday. He was on the couch in the living room reading the newspaper. His wife, Awon, was taking an afternoon nap. They had married three years ago. Now they were expecting their first child. Sunday afternoons were usually quiet. Being used to his demanding banking job, he wasn't used to staying idle. His love of reading continued, even though it was hard to find time. But that afternoon, an article in the opinion page of the newspaper caught his attention. The writer criticized the ongoing ceasefire agreement between the 'Naga rebels', as he referred to them, and the Government of India. What disturbed him more was the writer's description of the underground movement as a 'terror outfit'. He thought it revealed the mindset of the majority of the Indian people, who were ignorant of the real situation and accepted uncritically whatever the media reported. But he acknowledged that increasingly the passionate movement of the Nagas had become more of a nuisance not just to the Indian public but also to the Nagas themselves. It had been five years since the two leaders had come to India and more than ten years since the ceasefire agreement had been brokered. Yet nothing much had happened since then. The people kept waiting, but now their patience was running out.

He wondered if the Naga movement for sovereignty would eventually achieve its goal or would come to nothing. When such thoughts arose, he thought of Joyson. His cousin had joined Mysore University soon after completing his PhD. Even though he was cynical of any positive outcome because of factional strife within the Naga nationalist movement, Joyson kept himself informed about all the political developments back home. Perhaps he hoped to be proved wrong one day. That he wasn't born a cynic was clear because he was always searching for something, even though he wasn't sure what it was. He became disillusioned and depressed only when he read deeper into the Naga problems, or the problems that the Nagas had brought upon themselves. Perhaps his scholarly research had led him to see things in a different way. Rakovei wondered if Joyson regretted being a research scholar sometimes, forced to analyse and re-analyse every given situation. Did he ever wish he could be like the majority of people at home, ignorant but hopeful? Perhaps there were times when he did.

Rakovei would call his cousin once in a while, especially when he wanted to talk about the problems confronting their people. Their conversation invariably turned to the ongoing Indo-Naga political talks or the rising menace of the ceasefire-empowered underground cadres who had now become the bosses, roaming around towns and increasingly becoming a hindrance to freedom. Their Delhi days had strengthened the cousins' bond. Besides, Joyson maintained that only a few people shared the same 'Wave length'—whose thoughts were similar. In effect, Rakovei was a sounding board for Joyson's ideas and analyses. Gradually, things seemed to be unfolding along the lines predicted by Joyson. He had strongly believed that Isak and Muivah's acceptance of the invitation to come to India for talks was a mistake. He had always held that the Naga leaders were ignorantly playing into the hands of Indian intelligence.

'Look what India is doing,' he had said a few years back. 'From drafting the agreement to negotiating at the highest level, the prime ministerial level, to being slowly pushed to the level of a home secretary. It's just a matter of time before this whole Naga issue will be swept under the carpet to be forgotten. The talks will fade away on their own.'

But then, Rakovei thought, the frequent change of guard at the centre had also contributed to the derailing of the peace process. Even though some people did not like to question the sincerity of the Government of India's effort to resolve the Naga problem, the frequent shuffling of governments and the transfer of officials at the centre had hampered the smooth progress of the negotiations. Besides, each party in power at the centre had different opinions on the Naga issue. Certainly, India had too many other problems to deal with. And so along the way and with time, the attention paid to the Naga issue dwindled away. Had the Nagas failed to take the opportunity when it was offered to them? It seemed wishful thinking now, Rakovei thought, but had the Naga leaders been realistic and had they negotiated well with the Government of India when the first ceasefire was brokered in the 1960s, things would have been better. Instead, they had turned away, thinking that they had nothing to do with India. Or had they been waiting to receive a bigger slice of a pie that was never there? Sovereignty—that was a big word now. It no longer appeared in the talks. Or rather, India wasn't willing to use the word. So where were the Nagas headed to now?

The ordinary people at home kept waiting, but now even they knew that something wasn't quite right. Certainly, they knew how to read the signs. They were no longer willing to accept false promises made by the underground leaders. People were no longer ignorant. Once they had been happy accepting whatever was given to them, but now that was no longer the case. They distrusted those who had once given them information. When they saw the lives of their leaders, they knew something had really gone wrong. Once the underground workers were lovingly called 'national workers', but now people were reluctant to use the phrase. Ever since they had come above ground following the ceasefire agreement, many had gone wayward. Perhaps life out in the open was too much for them to handle and they had become floating bodies, obstructing everyone's way. Rakovei encountered the harsh new reality for the first time when he went home for Christmas the year before he got married. The drunkards on the street of Senapati town weren't the former good-for-nothing middle-aged men who had nothing to do. Now the drunks were the new men, the younger and violent undergrounds with guns. Nobody could challenge them. They had become a nuisance, his parents said, extorting money from everyone in the name of 'taxation' by the underground government. His biggest shock was seeing many underground cadres who had become suddenly rich. Senapati town had also grown rapidly. These undergrounds had got huge amounts of money from somewhere and had begun to invest in the growing businesses of the town. Several multi-storey buildings had come up on the low-lying old highway. He pointed to one and asked his mother who owned the property. He thought it must be someone who was born rich. He was shocked when she said it belonged to an uncle from their own village. He remembered the first time he had seen the uncle. At the time, he was a wretched young underground cadre, thin and hungry and wet. He could still recall the scene.

It was the summer when he went home for *Laonüh*, the year of Operation Bluebird. One rainy day, when he was home with his grandmother, some underground soldiers walked past their house. One of them stepped onto the veranda and knocked on the door. He wanted to greet Grandmother. She was obviously not expecting anybody to visit that afternoon. Young Rakovei crept outside with Grandmother to see who it was. The youth before them was wearing a pair of olive green trousers and black boots. Though drenched from head to toe, he didn't seem to be bothered. Perhaps he was used to it. His upper body was covered with a sodden *teisa*, the traditional black shawl with red and green lines on the border. Under the shawl he was carrying a rucksack. The sounds of clanging utensils could be heard from his rucksack. Given that they were always on the move, the undergrounds carried their possessions with them wherever they went.

Unsure how to greet the unexpected visitor, Grandmother said, 'Goodness me! I'm unprepared for a visitor at this time. What can I give you?'

'That's all right, aunty,' the young cadre said. 'I have to catch up with my friends, so I will hurry along. But I didn't want to pass your house without saying 'hello'. I hope everything is well with you.'

'Yes, I'm well. Where are you all headed?' Before he could answer, Grandmother motioned for him to wait. She disappeared into the kitchen, a multi-utility room used for storing grains and also as a chicken coop. She returned with two eggs and gave them to the young man. 'Take these. The hen just laid them. They are warm. Just gulp them down. They will give you some energy along the way. I don't have anything else to give you.'

'Thank you, aunty.' He accepted the eggs gratefully and ran to join his friends.

'Poor boy, he must be having a hard time,' whispered grandmother, looking into the distance where the young man and his friends had disappeared into the mist and the rain. She said he had joined the underground movement at a young age, after dropping out of school. Grandmother felt sorry for the young cadre because his mother had died early and his father had remarried. His inability to fit into the new family was also what compelled him to leave home and join the underground. But that was almost twenty years ago. Now the once-pitiable youth had become a wealthy man, living a lavish life. Though he wasn't educated, his long service in the underground organization had earned him a comfortable position. But certainly that alone wasn't enough to explain the lifestyle he was living.

Where did he get so much money, Rakovei wondered, still picturing the wretched young man he had encountered several years back. Soon enough, however, he began to hear about the ways in which the former underground cadres made money. Within a few years of coming out to live in the larger society, many had begun poking their noses into everything, and turned to extortion. They terrified the common folk, who didn't understand how the situation had changed. As time passed, many of these underground cadres became more and more reckless and emboldened. Before the ceasefire, they had been in the jungle, hiding from the Indian armed forces. Now, with the ceasefire agreement in place, they had licence to roam about freely, with their pistols tucked into the waistband of their trousers or under their arms. Was it part of the deal that they could be the bosses wherever they went? Was this the kind of freedom they had been fighting for?

Of course, there were still a good number of sincere cadres who continued to lead humble lives and waited patiently for better times to come. But they were easily outnumbered, and their silence was drowned by the recklessness and bravado of the many unruly cadres. The younger men, especially the newer recruits, were after creature comforts, and did not really understood what the organization stood for.

Despite the ceasefire, recruitment for the movement continued. Surprisingly, the response was even better because everyone knew the jungle life was over, now that the ceasefire had been extended indefinitely. Many rowdy youngsters who were mostly social misfits were now being recruited. They were uncontrollable, and the higher authorities in the organization weren't doing much to control these wayward cadres, who were increasingly defining the image of the organization.

Public anger was increasingly focused on the badly behaved former undergrounds, whose 'tribe' was increasing with time. The former 'freedom fighters' were now 'rebels without a cause'. Many young people in the movement did not know what they were fighting for.

The leaders tried to placate the public by promising to handle the wayward cadres, but they did nothing. The same people, in the name of the underground groups, continued to run rampant, serving extortion-taxation letters to ordinary people and threatening them with dire consequences if they did not agree to their demands. It was difficult to tell if they were merely following orders from the higher authorities or if they were acting on their own. The public was disillusioned. There was a time when people donated their hard-earned money to the movement that promised to bring them freedom and dignity. Now people only gave money out of fear. The public was silent only because they knew that these upstarts would not hesitate to kill them. Once the people had feared the Indian army, but now they were afraid of the bullets of the undergrounds. To die at the hands of their own people would be a bigger tragedy. In the past, even ordinary people proudly bore pain and suffering and torture, or died for the cause of the Naga nation, but now they were dying for no reason.

Rakovei thought about Uncle Lenny. What did he think about all these changes? Did he feel that he had suffered pain for nothing, that he had defended the 'freedom fighters' for nothing? What did people who had suffered torture like him get in the end? Only pain and suffering.

Twenty years had passed since the Oinam incident and Operation Bluebird, but the bitter memories still remained. The wait for justice continued. In the first few years, NPMHR and some other human rights organizations filed several cases with the Gauhati High Court against the Assam Rifles for human rights violations during Operation Bluebird, including charges of killing, torture, illegal arrest and detention and destruction of property. Even though the High Court ordered inquiries into the allegations, nothing substantial resulted. Nor was any compensation paid to the victims. The Indian armed forces were too powerful to be brought before the court of law. After all, they had AFSPA to protect them. Several agitations calling for the repeal of the notorious Act had been held, but they had all fallen on deaf ears. The indefinite fast for the repeal of the Act by Irom Sharmila Chanu since 2001 had brought fresh attention to the atrocities committed by the army in Manipur. Yet Manipur was too far away for the larger Indian public to bother about, so that even the death-defying act of the young woman was confined to a news item and the seriousness of the act was hardly appreciated. Ten years after the Oinam incident, the ceasefire agreement was signed. But the first major technical snag occurred when the ceasefire was extended 'beyond territorial limits'. This didn't go down well with the Meiteis of the Imphal valley. As a result, the valley flared up, forcing the Government of India to retract its steps while the Naga underground government mutely watched what was happening.

Rakovei wondered if a viable solution would ever be found to the Naga political conflict. Given the current political situation, he couldn't see any signs of the political stalemate ending in the near future. It took a lot to hope for a better tomorrow, a tomorrow that would usher in peace. The young generation of today was not willing to wait, like their parents and grandparents had. But what were the chances of achieving peace? On such days, when thinking about the Naga political question, he wanted to write articles and send them to newspapers. He had even written a couple of them. But when he read them later, he realized that he was too biased against the underground movement. Perhaps his opinion was excessively influenced by the more recent turn of events at home. Besides, he was also in a difficult situation because of his father-in-law's position in the movement. Speaking against the ugly side of the movement would put him directly in opposition with his wife's family.

Lost in thought, Rakovei didn't realize the room had become dark. He switched on the lights. Standing by the window, he looked outside. Darkness was slowly descending and soon the street lights would come on. The distant hazy view of the city suddenly reminded him of his childhood when he used to play carefree in the dust by the roadside near his home. He was overcome by nostalgia for his childhood years, years that would never come back. He drew the curtains, as though trying to shut out both his thoughts as well as the outside world. But he was successful in blocking out only the world outside the window. His mind wouldn't stop working and thinking and wondering. He felt he was living between hope and despair.

Acknowledgements

The realization of this novel has been quite a journey—from the initial excitement of building it from the skeleton in my mind to disappointments midway for fear of not being published to picking up the pieces...I have quite a bunch to thank.

Easterine Kire, you've not allowed me to give up on this one. I cannot thank you enough. You're one of the humblest human beings I've met and a very persistent one too!

Preeti Gill, thank you for making this happen! You're truly a 'gentlewoman'! And thank you for connecting me to Malini Sood. Thank you Malini for cleaning up the mess of a manuscript!

Hansda Sowvendra Shekhar, thank you for offering to write a blurb. You're such a generous soul!

Ravi Singh and the entire team at Speaking Tiger—thank you so much for agreeing to publish this piece of work.

Sanjoy Hazarika, thank you for the advice on the improvement of the novel.

Thanks to my friends—Lumreiphy (Alumphy) Raikhan, Shelmi Sankhil, Nzanmongi (Jasmine) Patton, Senganglu (Sengmei) Thaimei—for reading the unrefined manuscript patiently and giving valuable feedback.

Thank you to the big extended family of in-laws, for boosting my morale while 'waiting for Godot!' Godot has finally arrived! This wouldn't have endured the long wait if it wasn't for the encouragement you offered.

My dearest 'trio'—'sweetheart' Ashuni and the two little 'storytellers', Debbie and Joy—this is for you! I love you!

Thank you to all those have professed faith in me to bring this out, and have persistently asked about the progress of the novel!

God bless you all!